Looking After Our Land

Soil and Water Conservation in Dryland Africa

Will Critchley
edited by Olivia Graham

LOOKING AFTER OUR LAND:
Soil and Water Conservation in Dryland Africa
by Will Critchley
Edited by Olivia Graham

Published by Oxfam on behalf of the Arid Lands Information Network and
the International Institute for Environment and Development.

Oxfam
274 Banbury Road
Oxford OX2 7DZ
UK

First published 1991

British Library Cataloguing in Publication Data
A CIP catalogue record for this book is available from the British Library.

ISBN 0 85598 170 9

All photographs are by Will Critchley unless otherwise credited.

ALIN/IIED would like to express their sincere thanks to
the donors who funded this publication and its accompanying video.

COMIC RELIEF
EDWARD CADBURY CHARITABLE TRUST
OVERSEAS DEVELOPMENT ADMINISTRATION
OXFAM
SWEDISH RED CROSS

Project Steering Committee:
Will Critchley
Ced Hesse
Olivia Graham
Katharine McCullough
Camilla Toulmin

Designed by Bob Prescott Design Associates
Printed by Oxfam Print Unit
Illustrations by Timothy Critchley

Both this book and the accompanying video are available in English and French and can be obtained through
Oxfam country offices as well as direct from:

Oxfam Publications, 274, Banbury Road, Oxford OX2 7DZ, U.K.

Drylands Programme, IIED, 3 Endsleigh Street, London WC1H 0DD, U.K.

ALIN/RITA, Casier Postal 3, Dakar-Fann, Senegal.

INTRODUCTION   I

**PART ONE: OVERVIEW –
LEARNING FROM EXPERIENCE**

PART TWO: CASE STUDIES

PART THREE: TECHNICAL SECTION

FIGURES FOR TECHNICAL SECTION

INTRODUCTION

"Desertification" is not the creation of a desert – or very rarely! It is a process of resource degradation. Helping people to acquire the tools, knowledge and confidence they need to reverse this process is one of the major challenges facing development workers in arid and semi-arid Africa.

Soil conservation projects in sub-Saharan Africa have had a troubled record over the past 30 years or so, and their failure has had extremely serious consequences, especially for those people living in the dryland areas.

Two main factors have contributed to the failure of these projects. First, for marginal farmers, the idea of "preventing future loss of soil" is irrelevent to present needs, and second, the farmers themselves have, in the past, simply not been consulted about their knowledge and understanding of the processes of erosion. Both traditional technology and social organisation have usually been ignored, and solutions have been imposed from above. This has led to such "solutions", even where they show some technical merit, never being taken up with enthusiasm by local communities and fading into oblivion when the project itself finishes.

However, in the last decade a number of interesting developments have taken place. With the help of a handful of projects, people across Africa have demonstrated that they are motivated, competent and capable of taking charge of their environment and its protection. There is strong and growing evidence that when local communities are sufficiently involved in planning and implementation, these soil and water conservation activities can be, and are sustained beyond the life of the initiating project.

In late 1989, the Arid Lands Information Network based at Oxfam and the Drylands Programme at IIED shared their growing concern at the very small amount of resource material on soil and water conservation being produced by and for development workers at project level despite the great demand for relevent information. ALIN and IIED decided to collaborate on the production of a video with accompanying notes to try to fill the gap. The 'accompanying notes' turned into a book... and here it is.

This book is about the main lessons to be learnt from new approaches to soil and water conservation in sub-Saharan Africa. It presents six case studies, two each from Burkina Faso, Kenya and Mali, where soil and water conservation, based on the participation of the local people, has resulted in some success. The book brings out the essential ingredients of a successful soil and water conservation project and provides a set of questions which should be asked before embarking on such a programme – not a fixed list of steps to take, but some important points to remember.

The fieldwork for the book was carried out during 1990, and descriptions of project work and progress therefore obviously relate to the projects at that stage.

It is written expressly for development workers in arid and semi-arid Africa, on whose experience it is based. Together with the accompanying video (90 mins) it is suitable for use in workshops or discussion groups as well as being of more general interest to a wider audience concerned with environmental issues. It also stands on its own as a useful reference tool.

PART ONE

Learning from Experience

1. NEW APPROACHES TO OLD PROBLEMS

First we look at the reasons for the past failure of most soil and water conservation projects in East and West Africa. What went wrong with so many of them, in spite of their good intentions?

SOIL CONSERVATION PROJECTS – WHY SO MANY FAILURES?

Concern about soil conservation is nothing new in Africa. Several colonial administrations recognized that there was an erosion problem early this century. In the British-ruled territories soil conservation became a major issue during the 1930s, when a number of schemes were started. Programmes of one sort or another continued in most countries until independence. But the majority of these schemes were resented by the local people, who were forced to supply labour.

Few of the bunds and terraces constructed were maintained by the "beneficiaries" afterwards. Soil conservation was seen as being a form of colonial oppression. It is not surprising then that independent Governments found it difficult at first to support soil conservation programmes. When conservation projects did begin to reappear, many of the same old mistakes were made again. Until very recently there has been a long list of soil conservation failures.

Historical failures have been discussed in two of the case studies. In Machakos District of Eastern Kenya, soil conservation work was made compulsory under the colonial administration and forced labour was used for community conservation programmes. Although some of the techniques were effective, the methods used were very unpopular.

The second example comes from Burkina Faso, where the "GERES" project of the 1960s was another failure. In this case, machinery was used to construct terraces over whole catchments. But the work was done without any attempt to involve the local people in planning. The bunds were simply ignored when the machinery had finished, and nothing was maintained.

> **SOME OF THE CAUSES OF FAILURE:**
> - compulsory labour under colonial rule
> - unpopular rules and regulations to enforce conservation
> - centralised planning by experts
> - planning on the basis of geographical "catchments" rather than natural village units of land
> - use of heavy machinery which it was not possible to maintain
> - structures which needed very large amounts of labour
> - too much emphasis on soil erosion rather than conservation of moisture for plant productivity

THE GROWING NEED FOR EFFECTIVE CONSERVATION PROGRAMMES

The need for conservation programmes is much greater now than when the first unpopular programmes were started!

Population has increased. This means that more land has to be used for cultivation, and fields cannot be rested from cropping to recover their fertility as in the past. Another result of the growing population has been the increasing need for firewood. Often more wood is used than is produced. The system has slipped out of balance.

Livestock numbers in many areas have increased and the animals are squeezed on to less and less land as cropping expands. Inevitably the vegetative cover of grass and bush suffers – particularly in dry years.

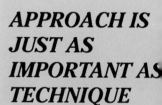

APPROACH IS JUST AS IMPORTANT AS TECHNIQUE

GROWING POPULATIONS HAVE LED TO AN INCREASED NEED FOR FIREWOOD, BURKINA FASO.

FARMERS ARE PART OF THE SOLUTION NOT PART OF THE PROBLEM

CREDIT: Olivia Graham/OXFAM

TECHNIQUES WHICH LEAD TO RAPID YIELD INCREASES ARE THE MOST POPULAR.

Rainfall has decreased. Rainfall remained below average after the droughts of the late 1960s and 1970s. Areas which used to produce good yields in most years became "marginal" for growing crops. Sorghum areas became millet areas.

In recent years, growing populations, and increased needs for firewood and farming land, combined with reduced rainfall, have led in many areas to land degradation – in other words the land can no longer support the same amount of crops, grass, trees or livestock as before. In extreme cases, land which used to produce good vegetation is now bare and hard.

One vital difference between the situation in the present day and the situation twenty or thirty years ago, is that now without some sort of soil and water conservation, many of the farmers in the dry zones simply cannot continue to produce crops, or feed their animals.

People are deeply concerned, and in many areas they are ready to respond to conservation programmes – if the programme makes sense.

In each of the six areas studied, there is a similar basic problem – how can land be kept productive? And in extreme cases, how can land that has become barren be brought back into productivity?

NEW APPROACHES – SOME SUCCESS AT LAST

Recently there have been some hopeful signs that conservation projects can meet with success. This means:

- the measures carried out are *effective*
- they are *appreciated* by the local land users

and... the final proof...

- the systems are actually *adopted* by the community and put into practice voluntarily.

There is one common theme which runs through all of the projects where there are signs of success. It is **POPULAR PARTICIPATION,** and it is perhaps the most important lesson of all.

There are other common factors too. The projects which can claim some success tend to be fairly small scale. They treat farmers as part of the solution, rather than part of the problem, by working closely with them and trying to promote techniques which are easy to understand and simple to carry out.

One very important characteristic of all the successful projects is that they have developed techniques which give farmers a rapid yield increase – based on conservation of moisture rather than just soil. This is the priority in dry areas.

Many countries in sub-Saharan Africa found it politically impossible to support soil and water conservation programmes soon after independence. But now there are signs in certain countries that there is a political will for conservation to succeed.

A WORD OF CAUTION!

We should not get carried away with the success stories and assume that conservation programmes have changed radically from the old days. This is unfortunately not the case! There are still plenty of projects with mistaken approaches which continue to spend a lot of money, building many kilometres of structures by machine or under food-for-work schemes without having any thought for what happens when the project comes to an end.

Even with the most successful projects there is still a long way to go before we can say that the majority of the land is "conserved". There is still a huge gap between what has been achieved and what could be achieved. It will take a lot of commitment from the people, the development workers, the donors and the Governments to reach this goal.

However some light can be seen at the end of the tunnel. The purpose of this booklet is to look at some of the successes in detail, and to analyse why things have worked, and what hope there is for the future.

MALI

Projet Lutte Anti-Erosive (PLAE): Koutiala

Tree planting is part of the PLAE programme

Traditional Soil and Water Conservation: Dogon Plateau

Dogon village

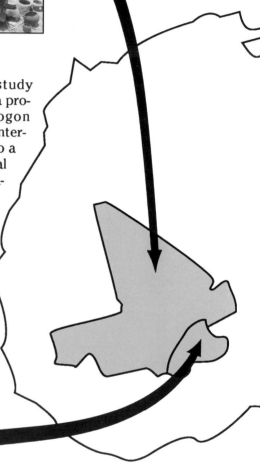

PLAE is the largest and oldest conservation project in Mali. It is situated in the relatively wet part of southern Mali, but degradation is nevertheless a problem here also. PLAE introduced the concept of village land-use management, planned and coordinated by village associations. A range of erosion control techniques have been introduced – some more successfully than others.

This is the only case study which does not involve a project directly. The Dogon Plateau is of particular interest because it is home to a wide variety of traditional soil and water conservation measures. There can be few other areas in sub-Saharan Africa where the local people have devised such a range of conservation techniques. The measures could be improved, but there is much to learn from them.

BURKINA FASO

Participation is one of PAF's strengths.

Projet Agro-Forestier (PAF): Yatenga Province

The Agro-Forestry project (PAF) has built up the reputation of being one of the most successful soil and water conservation projects in sub-Saharan Africa. PAF promotes contour stone bunding and planting pits as its main conservation technique. Participation of the local farmers in all aspects of the project and a very well organised training system are PAF's main strengths.

Lorries are used by PATECORE to help farmers transport stones.

PATECORE: Bam Province

PATECORE is a recent conservation project on Burkina Faso's Central Plateau. PATECORE has set up a provincial committee for the coordination of development activities and promotes self-help by local communities. Communities are encouraged to develop village land-use management plans, and are trained to use aerial photographs for this purpose. Permeable rock dams are the project's most important conservation activity.

CREDIT: Jeremy Hartley/OXFAM

For the case studies we visited three countries, Burkina Faso, Kenya and Mali, and studied two areas in each. We tried to cover very different projects in contrasting situations. The idea was to highlight experiences from as wide a range of dryland areas as possible.

This is a brief introduction to the case studies which will be referred to in the next section. Part 2 of the book takes each area/project in turn and describes it in detail.

KENYA

The National Soil and Water Conservation Project (NSWCP): Machakos District

In Machakos District, much of the work is carried out by self-help mwethya groups.

Machakos probably has the best soil and water conservation record of any district in Kenya. Though rainfall is quite high on average, lack of moisture for the crops and erosion are both serious problems. However most of the arable land has now been terraced. Success has largely depended on the self-help groups which implement much of the conservation. The farmers, many of whom are women, have recognised the benefits of terracing.

The Lokitaung Pastoral Development Project (LPDP): Turkana District

Oxen-drawn scoops make earth moving easier.

LPDP is situated in a remote area of northwest Kenya. This is an arid and difficult area where there is a history of hardship and relief food aid. The people are mainly semi-nomadic pastoralists. The programme began as a water harvesting project but has now become a long-term development programme, mostly concerned with pastoral production – the main occupation of the local people. LPDP is managed by the people themselves.

2. THE LESSONS

What are the essential ingredients of a successful soil and water conservation project? This is the heart of the book. Let's take a close look at the most important messages from the case studies.

PARTICIPATION

Participation of the local people in all stages of project activity is the most important lesson of all. It is the voluntary cooperation that has grown up within communities which has made the difference between the few conservation projects which have met with some success, and the many which failed.

It ought to be obvious that the people themselves have to be involved in the projects! Without their support, whatever is done from outside is doomed to failure. This is not only because systems have to be maintained, but also because no project on its own can cover all of the area which needs conserving.

Participation takes many forms and has several stages. We will see in the lessons that follow that it is stressed time and time again. For example *training and motivation* includes involving the people in laying out and building the structures, and in *village land use management* the village groups take responsibility for their own land. When we talk of *suitable systems*, this means systems that can be implemented and maintained by the people with the minimum support from outside.

People need to be involved in conservation projects from their very beginning and during all the following stages:

- planning of the project's targets and objectives
- land use planning
- technical training
- designing and building the structures
- maintenance of the systems
- monitoring and evaluation

Each of the studies demonstrates the importance of participation.

In Burkina Faso, PAF has a particularly strong technical training programme for villagers, and PATECORE has developed a land use planning system where the community sets its own priorities for conservation activities. In Kenya, NSWCP in Machakos depends entirely on voluntary labour, usually by groups, to carry out the terracing work, and LPDP in Turkana has become, effectively, the people's own project. Finally in Mali PLAE has helped develop strong village associations which coordinate the conservation activities, and on the Dogon Plateau of course all the traditional soil conservation is carried out entirely by the local people without assistance.

> If a soil and water conservation project – or any other similar village project – is to succeed, it must win the respect and the cooperation of the local people.

THE FULL PARTICIPATION OF LOCAL PEOPLE IS CRUCIAL TO THE SUCCESS OF THE PROJECT. LPDP, KENYA.

8

SUITABLE SYSTEMS

There are many well-tested techniques for soil and water conservation which have been developed in Africa over the last 50 years, but they have two main weaknesses. First, many of them require very large amounts of labour – or even machines – for construction.

Second, most of the techniques are for the higher rainfall areas – where prevention of erosion is more important than conservation of moisture.

In the drier areas of sub-Saharan Africa we want techniques which will conserve or even harvest rainwater and which are simple and cheap. This is what is meant by suitable systems.

It is vital to remember that a number of techniques which work well in one area may not do so elsewhere, for various reasons. It is tempting to suggest that the contour stone bunds of PAF could be used all over the region... but in many areas there are simply not enough stones! The earth basins made by the Dogon are extremely effective in conserving every drop of rainwater... but in regions where animals are used for weeding, the basins would be destroyed. Many techniques are therefore site specific.

The PATECORE project in Burkina Faso has developed a water harvesting technique called permeable rock dams. This is a kind of structure which has been particularly designed for the sites found in this type of dry area – namely fertile valley bottoms, where water used to spread naturally, but which are now developing gullies in the middle. This technique can only be used where there is a good supply of stone – and where permeable rock dams are a local priority. As you can see, this technique is appropriate for the area around PATE-CORE, but will not be suitable for everywhere in sub-Saharan Africa.

The *fanya-juu* terraces of Machakos District in Kenya are the mainstay of the soil conservation project, NSWCP. This technique is ideal for Machakos, where there is relatively deep soil and high slopes, and the priority is to hold rainwater in place. It is well understood and appreciated by the local inhabitants.

One technique which has an indirect effect on soil and water conservation – by reducing the amount of fuelwood needed – is the improved cooking stove promoted under PLAE in Mali. This is an example of a technique which could be used almost everywhere.

TRADITIONAL HILLSIDE TERRACE ON DOGON PLATEAU.

TRAINING AND MOTIVATION

In the past, soil conservation projects have trained people to dig ditches, or build bunds. And that was where the training stopped! There was little attempt to help people understand how land became degraded or how to improve land management. Even these days many projects restrict technical training to project staff. The local people are often looked upon as being merely the beneficiaries – and a source of labour.

But now there is plenty of evidence to show that villagers can quickly understand what the environmental problems are and how they can be solved. Taking training a step further, villagers are taught new technical skills such as the use of simple surveying instruments. When techniques such as laying out contours are demystified, the people are brought right into the heart of the activities – and they become a part of the project.

PAF in Burkina Faso has a very well-developed training system for villagers. Originally, a model of a contour stone bund was used to demonstrate to trainees how runoff could be controlled in the field. Now, visits to neighbouring villages to see "the real thing" are used for the same purpose. Visitors from elsewhere in Burkina Faso, and even neighbouring countries come to see the contour stone bunds as well: exchange visits are very valuable!

PAF trains villagers to use the water tube-level to lay out contours. Within an hour or two the trainees are laying out contour lines in fields with a great deal of accuracy. It is extraordinary that some projects still use "high-tech" surveying equipment for the same purpose. PAF also trains villagers in the careful construction of bunds and explains the importance of each stage.

TRAINING PUTS SKILLS INTO THE HANDS OF THE PEOPLE

PLAE in Mali uses a system of training called the "GRAAP" method ("Groupe de Recherche et d'Appui pour l'Autopromotion Paysanne") which is an interactive form of education based on the visual aid of a flannelgraph. The villagers stick outlines of trees/stone bunds/gullies on a board and discuss the processes of erosion, and how to go about land-use planning. In addition, PLAE uses a series of slides which are shown to villagers to demonstrate the whole cycle of land degradation and conservation.

In Kenya's Machakos District, NSWCP trains self-help groups' leaders to lay out contours using the line level – an instrument similar to PAF's water-tube level. Training in soil and water conservation is even taken down to the level of primary-school children by the project.

A MODEL OF A CONTOUR STONE BUND IS USED TO DEMONSTRATE HOW RUNOFF CAN BE CONTROLLED. PAF, BURKINA FASO.

10

USING EXISTING GROUPS AND INSTITUTIONS

Groups are required in soil and water conservation and village land-use management projects for two main purposes. These are:

- the planning and coordinating of activities;
- the implementation and construction of conservation measures.

A clear lesson from several of the case studies, is that it is best to use existing groups for these activities. Such groups or institutions may be traditional, or may have been set up previously for another purpose. In any event an existing group is almost always easier to work with than one which has to be specially formed.

For planning, village associations of one form or another are the best organisations. Most villages (in West Africa) or sub-locations (in Kenya) have committees which meet regularly and could take responsibility for conservation planning.

For construction the picture is not so clear. In some areas people are used to working in groups – in others they are not. In some areas the groups are informal, and consist of friends and neighbours, in other areas there are formal working groups, registered with the government. But some people are not used to working communally at all – and efforts to make them form groups meet with failure. Groups are not always popular.

The best example from our case studies of active groups is in Machakos District in Kenya, the district where the National Soil and Water Conservation Project has been most successful. Here *mwethya* groups have been responsible for most of the terracing activities in the district. The groups terrace each member's farm in turn. The Ministry of Agriculture even uses the groups as "contact farmers" for its extension programme. The groups are traditional, but are now officially registered with the government. It is significant that outside Eastern Kenya, where such *mwethya* groups do not exist, the project has met with much less success – and it has not been easy to encourage other areas to form similar groups.

In Turkana District, also in Kenya, LPDP has based its management committees on traditional institutions which has given the project much credibility locally. However, the actual work is carried out by informal groups of friends – quite different from Machakos.

On the Dogon Plateau in Mali, construction of soil conservation measures has historically been done by individuals. However a new project has recently introduced the idea of paid group labour to speed up some of the more labour-demanding tasks.

SELF-HELP MWETHYA GROUPS HAVE DONE MOST OF THE TERRACING IN MACHAKOS DISTRICT KENYA.

WORK WITH EXISTING GROUPS

FLEXIBILITY

Some of the main lessons in the book do not only apply to soil conservation. They are equally true for other types of projects. The need for flexibility is one example. What we mean by flexibility is the willingness and ability of a project to alter its workplans in response to its experience and to people's priorities.

Anyone who has worked on a project, whether a small NGO project or a large multilateral operation, knows that they rarely end up looking like their preparatory documents had planned. And yet there is always pressure on the project staff to achieve targets – targets which often turn out to be entirely unrealistic. The danger is that the project pushes programmes which the people don't want in order to stick to work plans.

The word "flexibility" may seem to imply weakness. In fact it is a strength. It is evolution. If flexibility is written into a project, the project is able to respond to changing circumstances without seeming to have failed! Workplans should always allow for reviews, and changes of direction. There should ideally be funds which are not tied to specific activities which can be used for items or activities which were overlooked during project preparation. At the very least a project should be prepared to change when change is necessary.

Lokitaung Pastoral Development Project in Kenya has modified its objectives so much that it needed to change its name!

The project started life as the Turkana Water Harvesting Project, and for the first three years of its life, concentrated on water harvesting for sorghum production. However the project management committee – composed almost entirely of the local beneficiaries – decided recently that the project had achieved its initial objectives and should now assist the people with their main priority, their livestock. The project has responded.

The Agroforestry Project (PAF) in Burkina Faso didn't change its name... but right from the start it was realised that an agroforestry project was not wanted in the area! The people made their priorities clear. They wanted help with food production, not tree planting. So PAF became a soil and water conservation/water harvesting programme. Only now, after more than ten years, is PAF becoming involved in agroforestry as part of its evolution into a village land-use management project.

In Mali, PLAE admits that not all of the techniques proposed worked well, and some were unpopular. So the project responded by making modifications. For example an earth bund/ waterway system was found to actually cause erosion, and so it was replaced by a more effective technique.

> Flexibility and the willingness to let a work programme evolve is a positive characteristic in any project. It is not a weakness.

ONLY NOW, TEN YEARS LATER, IS PAF BECOMING INVOLVED IN AGROFORESTRY

FLEXIBILITY IS STRENGTH

TRADITIONAL ONION TERRACES

BASING TECHNIQUES ON TRADITIONAL SYSTEMS

We have already noted the importance of using soil and water conservation techniques which are appropriate to each area. One approach is to find out what the people have done traditionally, and to work on improvements to those systems.

This approach has very seldom been used – though there are some interesting exceptions to talk about here. Indeed most soil conservation experts display a rather surprising ignorance of traditional techniques, which they either do not notice, or deliberately ignore!

This is a mistake. Many traditional techniques for soil and water conservation are in fact quite effective. Others were effective in the past, when conditions were different – when land was rested for longer, and rainfall was better. But unfortunately not enough is known about traditional soil and water conservation in Africa. This is rather an embarrassing admission for the "experts"!

On the Dogon Plateau there is a rich heritage of traditional techniques of soil and water conservation. Some of the techniques are growing in popularity, others are used less these days. Some may even have been introduced fairly recently. The systems are not perfect and there are a number of improvements which could be suggested. But the fact remains that the techniques are

remarkably ingenious – and yet have seldom been studied by any of the people who advise on conservation in the Sahel. There are lessons waiting to be learnt on the Dogon plateau.

PAF in Burkina Faso has done exactly as has been suggested above. The project has based its main technique, stone bunding, on the traditional system of simple stone lines. PAF has taken the basic system and improved it – by introducing the idea of contouring, and by building the bunds more carefully. In addition, PAF has revived the system of deep, widely spaced planting pits or *zai*, which improve the system further by collecting and concentrating rainwater. There has been no problem with acceptance of the two techniques by local farmers.

In Kenya the approach of LPDP has been rather different. Although its conservation/water harvesting developments are sited on existing plots, traditionally bunding did not exist. However there had been considerable experience in the district with water harvesting schemes. LPDP simply took its pick of the most successful techniques from other projects – and improved on them. Learning from other's technical experience is always worthwhile.11

> It is always worth studying traditional techniques of conservation and basing new systems on improvements of these, wherever possible.

VILLAGE LAND-USE MANAGEMENT

Soil and water conservation was conventionally thought of as being a series of structures – earth terraces or stone bunds for example – put in place to conserve a certain area of land. In fact effective conservation must be much more than that. In order for the problems of land degradation to be solved, there must be a wider or more "global" approach. This type of approach is some times called village land-use management.

What is village land-use management?

It is basically a system in which a village takes responsibility for all the land which is used by its inhabitants. While the privately cultivated fields are treated by individuals, the common lands are the responsibility of the village as a whole. This is one way of tackling the most difficult question of all – how to prevent degradation of the common grazing lands.

A village land-use committee is an essential starting point. This committee should be made up of members of the community who are respected and well-motivated. Its job is to plan and coordinate action. The normal stages are:

- planning appropriate land use in the village
- selection of suitable techniques for each zone
- working out a time-table for implementation

PLAE in Mali has adopted a "global" approach to conservation from the beginning and has the widest range of techniques of any of the projects studied, including stone lines, grass strips, live fences, improved cattle pens, check dams, tree planting and improved stoves.

Fortunately for this project, there were already well-established village associa-

tions which could be used to plan and coordinate the land-use management activities. Planning of appropriate land use is carried out using the flannelgraph system of sticking cut-out images on a board, after a visit around the village lands with the technicians of the project has taken place.

PATECORE in Burkina Faso aims to promote village land-use management, and has developed a very effective technique of training the villagers to use aerial photographs to identify traditional land units. This is the basis for planning.

VILLAGERS ARE TRAINED TO USE AERIAL PHOTOS

PAF in Burkina Faso is also branching out into a broader approach. PAF has a very successful system of conservation for agricultural land, but has realised that this is not enough. The grazing lands in particular present a problem – so village land-use management is being introduced.

Village land-use management is an exciting new idea which takes soil and water conservation one step further than simple earth terraces or stone bunds. It is an integrated global approach to conservation in which the villagers take responsibility for all their land.

14

COLLABORATION BETWEEN ORGANISATIONS

Too many projects work independently – often without letting other projects, or even the Government services, know what they are doing. Workplans and reports are not circulated, and there is no attempt to meet to coordinate activities. The result is that there is often an overlap – projects effectively doing the same work in the same area. At the worst, there may be competition between projects. The local people become confused, and inevitably it is they who suffer.

A number of the projects we have studied have a deliberate policy of collaborating with other institutions. The best example is PATECORE in Burkina Faso, where the project has set up a provincial-level committee for coordination of development activities. PATECORE also provides training for the staff of other projects and Government services.

In the drier zones of Kenya, small non-governmental projects often do not bother to inform the Government what they are planning or what they have achieved. It is therefore good to note that LPDP has forged links with the Government's District Development Committee.

Collaboration between development organisations is essential, to avoid confusing the local people, and to ensure better planning and a more efficient use of resources.

INCENTIVES

There is a long-standing debate about the use of incentives for development activities! There are those who argue that people should always be paid (with cash, tools or food) because they are poor. On the other hand it is argued that few or no incentives should be given, because incentives tend to make people dependent on help.

In our case studies it is clear that the majority of projects feel that incentives should be given, yet kept to a minimum, and that the emphasis should be on "tools-for-work". In Machakos District in Kenya, the only free inputs are indeed tools – shovels, hoes, pickaxes and so on. Likewise PAF in Burkina Faso recognises that people are genuinely short of tools, and makes hand tools available to village committees for allocation.

None of the projects pays cash for work to be done. Neither is food-for-work used (though LPDP in Kenya has just phased it out as a matter of policy), as it is seen as a disincentive to voluntary participation – in other words people would simply refuse to continue to work without food rations.

Incentives can be very useful to assist people in soil conservation activities. Food-for-work and direct payment should be avoided wherever possible. Tools are a better choice.

MECHANISATION

The debate about mechanisation is similar to the debate about incentives. Is it right to introduce machinery, which may break down and prove impossible to maintain after the project comes to an end? On the other hand is it fair to deny people the use of technology which will make work easier and much faster?

STONES FOR BUILDING BUNDS CAN BE CARRIED BY DONKEY CART WHEN THE DISTANCE IS NOT TOO GREAT.

Here we have contrasting views. PATECORE in Burkina Faso argues that "erosion is faster than a donkey cart", and therefore justifies the free provision of lorries to carry stones to make permeable rock dams. PLAE in Mali prefers to encourage people to use donkey carts for the same purpose. They think it preferable that people should rely on their own resources. In Burkina Faso, PAF supplies donkey carts to people who will use them, but has bought a lorry also for situations where stone has to be carried long distances...

This is a difficult debate. The balance of opinion seems to be that mechanisation is best avoided, because of the problems of maintaining the machinery in the future. However, if machinery is used, it should be under certain conditions. For example it should be used only where it is needed, and for a limited period such as during a construction phase.

> Despite the obvious advantages of mechanisation there can be serious problems of maintenance after the project comes to an end.

LIFE OF THE PROJECT

Projects rarely achieve much in three years. Yet three years is a common project life. Usually projects need time to modify their plans according to experience. Three years is no more than an establishment period. To be of real use to the communities served, projects need to have a long-term commitment. But equally they cannot go on for ever! They should plan for an eventual withdrawal when the development processes they have started can continue without project support.

This is the message which comes across from the projects we have looked at. In fact many of the projects are effectively open-ended, and new phases are funded according to requirements. Ten years after PAF started, now that the basic conservation techniques are well understood and have been widely adopted by farmers, the project is considering which direction it should take next.

> The life of a project should not be so short that it has no chance to become truly effective. Equally projects should always plan for eventual withdrawal.

MONITORING AND EVALUATION

Development projects in sub-Saharan Africa, whether large or small, are notoriously bad at monitoring, evaluation and adequate reporting. And yet these processes are extremely important. How can we plan for the future if we don't know what has been achieved, and how people have benefited? The lesson from our case studies is that not one of them has a truly satisfactory system of monitoring and evaluation.

Often it is said that techniques are extremely beneficial to farmers – and therefore there is no need to measure the results – crop yields, for example. But if no measurements are made, how can two techniques be compared? And how can you tell if the benefits are greater than the costs?

Even two of the most successful soil and water conservation projects in sub-Saharan Africa have inadequate monitoring and evaluation systems. PAF in Burkina Faso has few data on yields from farmer's fields, and there is some doubt how reliable the figures are. In Kenya, NSWCP admits that it does not yet have enough knowledge of the benefits of terracing on yields and on the soil.

> Adequate monitoring and evaluation systems need to be included in every project in order to collect data for analysing the costs and benefits of various techniques.

RAPID BENEFITS FOR FARMERS

Each of the main techniques introduced by the projects we have studied has led to rapid benefits for the farmers. This is

KEEP RECORDS – MEASURE YOUR SUCCESS

DON'T EXPECT DRAMATIC RESULTS TOO QUICKLY

16

FARMERS WANT BENEFITS NOW

GOMBRAOGO OUEDRAOGO, HAPPY WITH HIS CROP.

because the techniques used have been for moisture conservation or water harvesting rather than erosion control. Since rainfall is scarce in most of the project areas, when moisture is conserved, yields are improved. And by conserving moisture – in other words keeping rainfall on the field – soil is automatically conserved as well.

The permeable rock dams of PATECORE in Burkina Faso are a water harvesting technique. Although gullies in the valley bottoms are healed by the dams, it is the spreading of floodwaters over the fields which makes it so attractive to farmers. The *fanya-juu* terracing under NSWCP in Machakos, Kenya, is a moisture conservation technique. Because rainfall is relatively good here, all that is needed is to hold rainwater where it falls – and yields are improved. Where there is no terracing, runoff carries the rainfall away and plants suffer.

THE POOREST ARE OFTEN THE HARDEST TO REACH

The emphasis on moisture conservation rather than soil conservation has led to rapid benefits in terms of improved crop yields in dry areas. This is popular with farmers!

REACHING THE POOREST

One lesson which comes from a number of the projects is that the poorest of the poor don't always benefit from project activities. It is of course much easier to help those who can help themselves – those who can make use of the training and incentives that the project supplies. But there may have to be special measures taken to reach the very poorest groups.

However it may not always be a project's policy to assist those groups. For example, LPDP in Turkana District of northern Kenya deliberately aims to help only those who are not totally destitute. The reason is that LPDP has limited resources, and it wishes to concentrate on those who can use the project as a stepping stone back into self-reliance. It is not a relief programme.

PAF in Burkina Faso, on the other hand, does intend to reach the poorest. However there is an indication that some families cannot make use of the project's assistance because of their poverty. They may not, for example, be able to feed a group to work on their fields. PAF tries to overcome this problem by making food loans available through village committees.

Special planning may be required if a project is to reach the poorest of the poor.

LDPD HELPS TURKANA LIKE EMMANUEL KAMARET BACK INTO SELF-RELIANCE.

3. PLANNING A SOIL AND WATER CONSERVATION PROJECT
QUESTIONS TO ASK AND THINGS TO REMEMBER

How should we go about planning a soil and water conservation project in one of the dry areas of sub-Saharan Africa? How can we be sure that the project will benefit people – and the benefits will last?

There is no easy answer, but based on the lessons drawn from the six case studies, here is a summary of the most important things to remember, and some of the questions we must ask ourselves. Use this as a check list!

First we will look at project organisation and management, and then we will consider technical points.

I. PROJECT ORGANISATION AND MANAGEMENT

• Participation

Have we got the respect and the cooperation of the local people – the "beneficiaries"?   YES ☐   NO ☐

Are we answering their "felt needs"?   YES ☐   NO ☐

Are we involving them in all stages of planning, implementation, monitoring and evaluation?   YES ☐   NO ☐

Participation is the key to a successful project.

• Training and Motivation

Are we using technology which is appropriate – such as simple surveying instruments?   YES ☐   NO ☐

Are we taking training needs seriously?   YES ☐   NO ☐

Training puts skills into the hands of the people.

• Existing Institutions

Are there traditional working groups?   YES ☐   NO ☐

Which local institutions are the strongest? _____

_____

_____

_____

Work with existing groups.

Which institutions could help with planning at the village level? _____

_____

_____

_____

18

• Flexibility

Does the workplan allow a modification in targets or a change in direction?　　YES ☐　　NO ☐

Are we ready to evaluate progress and make changes if necessary?　　YES ☐　　NO ☐

• Life of the Project

Have we planned for a long enough period of project activity?　　YES ☐　　NO ☐

Is there provision to extend the project if things take off slowly?　　YES ☐　　NO ☐

• Incentives

Do we have to use food-for-work? _____
_____
_____
_____

What appropriate tools or other inputs could be used instead? _____
_____
_____
_____

How can we assist people in their work without creating dependence? _____
_____
_____
_____

• Reaching the Poorest

Is the programme reaching the poorest people?　　YES ☐　　NO ☐

Can they afford the time or labour to make use of what is being offered?　　YES ☐　　NO ☐

How can we channel help to them more effectively? _____
_____
_____
_____

• Monitoring and Evaluation

Can we say exactly what the benefits of the programme are? **YES** ☐ **NO** ☐

Is there a plan to take measurements and record useful data? **YES** ☐ **NO** ☐

How can we use the information gathered? _____

_____

_____

_____

• Collaboration between Organisations

Have we made sufficient contact with other organisations/projects in the area? **YES** ☐ **NO** ☐

Have we discussed the workplan with the Government? **YES** ☐ **NO** ☐

Do we circulate our reports to the right people? **YES** ☐ **NO** ☐

II. TECHNICAL ISSUES

• Traditional Systems

Has anybody made a study of local practices? **YES** ☐ **NO** ☐

Are there any traditions of soil and water conservation in the area? **YES** ☐ **NO** ☐

How could such systems (if they exist) be improved? _____

_____

_____

_____

Keep records – measure your success.

Collaborate to avoid confusion.

Build on what people already know.

• Suitable systems

Are we introducing a technique appropriate to the area   YES ☐   NO ☐

Is it the **most** appropriate system for the local conditions?   YES ☐   NO ☐

Has it been tested locally by other projects?   YES ☐   NO ☐

• Rapid Benefits

Farmers want benefits now!

Does the technique improve productivity or make yields more reliable?   YES ☐   NO ☐

Is it a moisture conservation or water harvesting technique which will help provide the crops with more moisture?   YES ☐   NO ☐

• Mechanisation

Approach mechanisation with care. Think before you mechanise.

Do we really need machines?   YES ☐   NO ☐

Do the people have the means to maintain them in the future?   YES ☐   NO ☐

What are the alternatives?_____

_____

_____

_____

• Village Land Use Management

Conserving fields is only the starting point.

Is there a village committee ready to take responsibility and make plans for village land-use management?   YES ☐   NO ☐

Are there plans for grazing land and fuelwood supply?   YES ☐   NO ☐

How can the community be motivated to act collectively? _____

_____

_____

_____

21

PART TWO

Case Studies

● BURKINA FASO ●

Burkina Faso, in the West African Sahel, has a serious problem of environmental degradation. However there are now many projects designed to conserve or rehabilitate land for agricultural production.

The Central Plateau of Burkina Faso has a high population density and suffered badly from the serious droughts of the 1970s and 1980s. Much of the land is eroded or degraded, and it is hard for the people who live there to produce sufficient food.

We have chosen two projects from Burkina to illustrate some of the ways in which these serious problems are being tackled.

These are:
• the Agroforestry Project (PAF) based at Ouahigouya, Yatenga Province
• the PATECORE Project based at Kongoussi, Bam Province

While there are a number of similarities between the two projects – for example they both promote techniques based on stone, and try to involve local people as much as possible – there are also differences. Both are successful projects, yet in each case there are still problems to be overcome.

I. THE AGROFORESTRY PROJECT (PAF) – YATENGA PROVINCE

SUMMARY

The Agroforestry Project (PAF) of Yatenga Province, Burkina Faso, has built up the reputation of being one of the most successful soil and water conservation projects in sub-Saharan Africa. PAF promotes contour stone bunding and planting pits as its main conservation techniques. Stone bunding is based on a traditional technique for water harvesting. It is a method by which degraded land can be rehabilitated, and it leads to rapid improvements in crop yields. In its extension work, PAF collaborates with various Government services. Participation of the farmers in planning and implementation is a central objective of the programme. PAF has a remarkably successful training programme for field staff and villagers.

Name: Agroforestry Project
(Projet Agro-forestier)

Contact: Mathieu Ouedraogo,
Project Manager

Address: B.P. 200
Ouahigouya, Yatenga Province,
Burkina Faso

Status: Non-Government Organisation

Sponsor/Donor: OXFAM (Oxford, UK)

Date of Start: 1979

BACKGROUND

Yatenga Province lies on the Central Plateau of Burkina Faso, and has the double problem of high population density (70-100 people per square kilometre) and severely degraded land. Over 50% of the land is under cultivation these days and little or no fallowing is practiced. Much of the remaining land is eroded and encrusted with a hard cap. It cannot be cropped without being improved. Overgrazing adds to the problem. Locally these barren expanses of land are known as *zipeela*.

To make matters worse, the rainfall has decreased significantly from the long-term average of 720mm/annum to 440 mm within the last twenty years. Not only is the rainfall low, but it is also very unreliable.

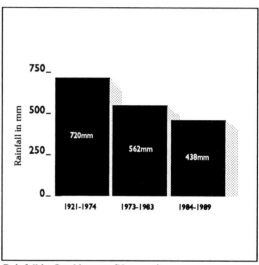

Rainfall in Ouahigouya (Yatenga)

Early efforts to improve land and increase cereal production were generally unsuccessful. In the 1960s, under a large scale, internationally funded project called GERES, heavy machinery was used to construct earth bunds over entire catchments – whether the land was used for agriculture or not. Work was carried out without any active participation by the local people.

The bunds were designed to drain rainfall runoff away from the fields to protect the soil from erosion. However, in subsequent years, when the rainfall diminished, this was the opposite of what the people wanted. They wanted the runoff on their fields to increase the moisture for their crops. The people didn't bother to maintain the GERES structures, and the bunds quickly lost their effectiveness.

ZIPEELA – BARREN ERODED LAND.

25

GERES failed because the people were not adequately consulted about their needs.

Environmental problems increased, and as the population grew and rainfall decreased in the 1970s and 1980s, the people were faced with a simple choice – to improve the land or to migrate.

In Summary:

- the population density is very high
- there are large expanses of barren land
- rainfall has diminished significantly over the last 20 years
- rainwater harvesting is required to grow crops well
- the people have to improve the land – or migrate

PAF'S APPROACH AND OBJECTIVES

When the Agroforestry project (PAF) began in 1979, it was, as its name suggests, an agroforestry project. It aimed to improve tree planting using "micro-catchment" techniques which collect rainfall runoff and concentrate it around tree seedlings. However it quickly became apparent that the people were not interested in planting trees. Their most urgent need was food production. As Mathieu Ouedraogo, the Project Manager, says:

"If you have a thorn in your foot and a thorn in your backside, which do you take out first? The thorn in your backside! Then you can sit down and remove the thorn in your foot!"

The moral of the story is "First things first!" PAF was flexible enough to change direction according to people's priorities.

Traditionally simple stone lines had been used to help reduce erosion in fields, but this practice had largely been forgotten. However through discussions with the people, PAF saw this as the basis for improved food production. The technique was resurrected and improved by building the stone lines along the contour. Contour stone bunds became the focus of the project's attention from 1982.

A contour is an imaginary line which runs along land of equal height above sea level. By building stone lines along the contour, rainfall runoff is spread behind the stone line and allowed to seep into the soil. This improves the amount of moisture for crops.

Having developed an effective technique, PAF's main role has been to motivate villagers, and then to provide appropriate training for them.

ACTIVITIES AND TECHNIQUES

1. Water Harvesting

PAF's main recommendation for the rehabilitation of degraded land, and improvement of existing cultivated land, is contour stone bunding. PAF took the rather crudely made traditional stone

CREDIT: Jeremy Hartley/OXFAM

CONTOUR STONE BUNDS – AN IMPROVEMENT ON THE TRADITIONAL TECHNIQUE.

lines and improved the design by aligning the bunds along the contour and building them more carefully. The contour is laid out by the use of a simple water-tube level (see technical section).

The new design allows the rainfall runoff to spread evenly through the field. When runoff reaches a stone bund, it spreads out and slowly trickles through the small holes between the stones. In addition, organic matter from the catchment area, such as eroded soil, bits of dead plants and manure, is filtered out of the runoff. This rich sediment builds up behind the bunds and this improves the soil.

In combination with stone bunds, another traditional technique called *zai* was reintroduced. *Zai* is the name in the local Moore language for wide and deep planting holes. The *zai* collect and concentrate runoff water for improved plant growth. Placing manure or compost in each *zai* further improves crop yields. Once again a traditional technique has been proved to have real value.

COMPOST IS PLACED IN EACH *ZAI* TO IMPROVE CROP YIELDS.

2. Village Land-Use Management

Recently PAF has broadened its outlook and has begun to promote the integrated approach of village land-use management. This approach gives the responsibility for conservation and development of village land to the villagers themselves. In certain villages special committees called "Village Land-Use Management Committees" have been set up. These committees look at the village land, decide what needs to be done to improve the whole area, and then coordinate the various conservation activities required, such as:

ZAI COLLECT AND CONCENTRATE RUNOFF WATER FOR IMPROVED PLANT GROWTH.

The combination of contour stone bunding and *zai* leads to rapid benefits for farmers. Yields are improved in the first season after the land has been treated, and even in very dry years these techniques ensure some yield. For these reasons the techniques have proved very popular, and by the end of 1989 some 8,000 hectares in over 400 villages had been treated with stone bunds.

THE PROJECT HAS ENCOURAGED THE LOCAL PRODUCTION OF COMPOST IN SPECIAL PITS.

- Stone bunding on a large scale.
- Compost pits.
- Enclosure of sheep and goats in the homestead.
- Village fodder plots.

27

THE PROJECT LORRY IS LOANED TO GROUPS WHEN TRANSPORT OF STONES IS A PROBLEM.

- Protection of communal land from overgrazing.
- Sowing Andropogon grass alongside stone bunds to form a vegetative barrier.
- Tree nurseries.
- Planting multi-purpose trees within the fields.

Although a number of the new techniques are not yet widely used, PAF is helping the people to see their potential by trying them out. From starting with two villages in 1989, by late 1990 the programme of village land-use management had spread to include eighteen villages.

PROJECT MANAGEMENT AND ORGANISATION OF WORK

1. Management of the Project

PAF has a small central office at Ouahigouya, with a total of 12 paid staff. Five of these staff are field extension agents, but PAF also works through the extension agents of three Government Services in Yatenga.

2. Organisation of the Conservation Work

The planning and coordination of conservation activities is carried out through village committees.

These committees are central to the programme. Before a village is allowed to join the programme, a committee must be set up. PAF's philosophy is that villages must develop their land resources themselves, through planning and coordination of self-help activities.

Conservation work is normally carried out by groups on a voluntary basis in fields belonging to members of the group. Food is provided for the group by the individual whose land is being treated. The type of group differs from village to village – some are more formal than others – but by and large PAF's experience has shown that groups work in Yatenga Province!

3. Incentives

PAF's philosophy is to use the minimum of incentives. The project believes that incentives should be used only where there is a specific need – a shortage of tools for example.

Incentives given to villagers to implement conservation measures include:

- pickaxes, shovels and wheelbarrows;
- donkey carts – for groups who buy their own donkeys;
- the loan of the project's lorry where the supply of stones is very limited and a large area has to be treated. In these instances the lorry is loaned free of charge to groups, but individuals are charged a small amount.

Additional help for the poorest farmers comes in the form of a food loan from the village committee, so that they can feed the group when work is done on their fields.

4. Participation

Full participation of the local people in all stages of planning and implementation is one of the strongest features of the project. Participation in the planning and organisation of activities takes place through the committees, and the work is carried out voluntarily by the people themselves.

TRAINING AND EXTENSION

PAF's training and extension system is the cornerstone of the programme's success.

PAF avoids the temptation to carry out its extension work independently, and joins hands with three Government services operating in the province. These are:

- the Regional Centre for Agropastoral Development
  (Centre Regional de Promotion Agropastoral – CRPA)

- the Provincial Office for the Environment
  (Direction Provinciale de l'Environnement Eaux et Forets – DPET)

- the Provincial Livestock Service
  (Service Provincial de l'Elevage – SPE)

PAF helps train the extension agents of these three services, who then collaborate in extension work.

Collaboration has led to more widespread achievements, and means that the activities should continue after the project comes to an end.

The project has developed a very effective training programme for farmers. PAF has trained thousands of farmers to use simple surveying equipment to lay out contours in the fields and to build improved bunds. Simple technology is within the reach of the villagers.

Training for villagers usually follows this sequence:

Stage 1: Extension agents from PAF and the other services (see above) meet villagers, and after a general discussion about conservation and development, a group of willing participants is selected for training.

Stage 2: Inter-village meetings and visits take place.

Stage 3: Training courses are held in the village.

The training courses consist of discussions about the need for conservation and land improvement. The main features of the courses are:

- using a model to demonstrate the effect of contour bunds (in the beginning, this was used a great deal, but is rarely needed now);
- training in the use of the water-tube level for surveying contours;
- construction of improved stone bunds.

A MODEL IS USED TO DEMONSTRATE HOW CONTOUR STONE BUNDS WORK.

By 1989 over 5000 people in more than 400 villages had been trained in this way, resulting in almost 8000 hectares of land being treated with stone bunds.

VILLAGERS ARE TRAINED HOW TO USE A WATER TUBE LEVEL

In recent years PAF has helped to train people from other regions of Burkina Faso, and also other countries. Visits to PAF by outsiders have become very common. During the first eight months of 1990 alone, fifteen groups from six countries visited the project.

YIELDS AND BENEFITS

The combination of contour stone bunds and *zai* can lead to significant yield increases – in the range of 40-60% – in the first season, and there is some evidence that yields may continue to increase for several seasons as fertile deposits are built up on the fields.

Most importantly, even in very dry years, treated fields yield some harvest. A survey in 1986 – a year of good rain – showed that whereas plots treated with stone bunds and *zai* yielded an average of 972 kg/ha, plots left untreated yielded an average of only 612 kg/ha.

However, as PAF admits, there is not yet enough accurate yield data to compare different areas or different years.

There is some concern that the benefits of PAF's interventions have not reached the very poorest farmers who are unable to provide food for group labour. It is for this reason that PAF has made food grain available to village committees, who can loan it to poor families to feed groups working on their fields.

PROBLEMS OUTSTANDING: WHERE NOW?

Degradation of Village Land

Improvements to private fields are not enough on their own, and each village must now take responsibility for halting degradation on all its land. Grazing areas pose a particular problem in this respect. The introduction of a village land-use management policy is intended to address this problem, and the first signs are that it is being accepted. However more motivation and training will be needed before the integrated approach can be fully effective.

Lack of Stone

The basic technique of stone bunding is excellent – as long as enough stone is available! But this is not always the case. PAF has recently bought a lorry to help transport stone long distances. The project also makes donkey carts available to those farmers who own or have access to donkeys. It is now faced with the dilemma of whether to buy more lorries or continue to promote the slower, but more appropriate, donkey transport.

Maintenance

The problem of what to do when the stone bunds become silted up – as they do after several seasons – is not yet satisfactorily answered. Where stone is plentiful, the bunds can be raised in height. But where stones are not available, one answer is to plant a grass (for example <u>Andropogon guyanus</u>) alongside the bund to act as a barrier hedge. However, it is difficult to grow these hedges thick enough to act effectively, and they take at least two seasons to develop well.

ANDROPOGON GRASS AND TREES ARE PLANTED ALONGSIDE STONE BUNDS TO ACT AS A BARRIER HEDGE.

Monitoring

Not enough is known about the effect of the techniques on crop yields and the reliability of harvests. The figures available show significant yield increases when stone bunding and *zai* are used together, but the data are not always of an acceptable scientific standard. PAF realises this, and is in the process of improving its monitoring system.

The Poorest Farmers

Is the project effectively helping the poorest of the poor? The achievements in terms of land treated are very impressive, but the majority of the farmers in

Yatenga have not yet bunded their fields. Why not? Is it just a question of time, or are there specific constraints, of labour for example? PAF is currently (1990) undergoing an evaluation, and this is one of the points which is being studied.

Withdrawal

Projects cannot last forever! Is it possible that activities could continue without PAF's help in some regions? Perhaps both inputs and training could be handled by experienced village committees with assistance from the Government development organisations. Should PAF be expanding, staying the same size or contracting?

LESSONS AND CONCLUSIONS

1. PAF is an internationally known success story. This is because of its impressive achievements and use of appropriate techniques. However the special combination of factors which make PAF so successful is not found everywhere in sub-Saharan Africa. PAF's techniques are rather site-specific.

2. Participation of villagers in decision making and in the implementation of soil and water conservation measures is central to PAF's philosophy and to its success.

3. Training and extension are among PAF's greatest strengths. PAF has a well developed training scheme for villagers during which they are taught how to lay out and build the bunds.

4. Flexibility in allowing the programme to evolve and change is a feature of the project. Having started as an agro-forestry project, PAF achieved considerable success with stone bunding techniques, and is now moving towards village land-use management.

5. The main technique, contour stone bunds with *zai* or planting pits, is simple, relatively cheap to implement and based on traditional techniques.

6. The techniques are particularly popular because they give farmers a rapid increase in crop yields, and allow at least some harvest in very dry years.

7. PAF is a small NGO project which is able to have an important impact on soil and water conservation by acting together with both government agencies and other NGOs.

Burkina Faso

EVERYONE PARTICIPATES IN CONSTRUCTING THE STONE BUNDS

SUMMARY

PATECORE is a conservation and land development project, based at Kongoussi on the Central Plateau of Burkina Faso. One of the project's first activities was to set up a provincial committee for the coordination of development activities. PATECORE promotes self-help by local communities and encourages discussion about development at all levels. Communities are encouraged to develop village land-use management plans, and are trained to use aerial photographs for this purpose. Permeable rock dams, which the local people feel to be a priority, are the project's most important conservation activity. Lorries have been introduced by the project free of charge to help farmers to carry stones for the construction of these rock dams.

Name: Projet Amenagement des Terroirs et Conservation des Ressources dans le Plateau Central (PATECORE)

Contact: Jean Bado Babou, Project Manager

Address: B.P. 271 Kongoussi, Bam Province, Burkina Faso

Status: Government Project – Ministry of Agriculture and Livestock (Ministère de l'Agriculture et de l'Elevage)

Sponsor / Donor: Ministry of Cooperation (German Government)

Date of Start: April 1988.

BACKGROUND

As with the Agroforestry project – PAF – in Yatenga, PATECORE is situated on the Central Plateau of Burkina Faso. The problems in Bam Province are similar to those of Yatenga. A growing population has caused increasing pressure on agricultural and grazing land, leading to abandonment of the fallow period in the fields and overgrazing of the common land. The result is land degradation due to over-use.

These problems have been made worse by the reduction in rainfall over the last 20 years. The annual average for the early part of the 1980s was as low as 500 mm – a very marked decline from the 1960s' when the average was nearly 700 mm.

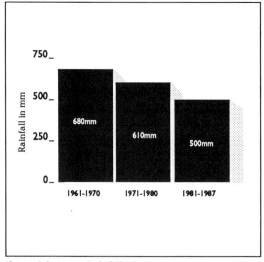

Annual Average Rainfall – Patecore

A particular problem around Kongoussi is the formation of gullies in the productive valleys where floodwaters previously used to spread naturally. Villagers rely on these valleys for crop production because the soil has been eroded away from the hillsides which they used to cultivate. The farmers have followed the soil, and the water, down from the hills!

Two national conservation projects, the "GERES" project of the 1960s and the "FEER" project of the 1970s/80s had programmes to combat land degradation. However their effect was limited by the lack of consultation or collaboration with the villagers.

GULLY NEAR KONGOUSSI

The problems:
- a growing population leading to increased pressure on land and other resources and consequent land degradation;
- marked decline of rainfall over the past twenty years;
- formation of gullies;
- lack of consultation with villagers by previous soil conservation projects.

The people's urgent priority now is to control the gullies in these valleys. One solution is permeable rock dams. These long, low structures rehabilitate the gullies and spread the floodwater. They improve plant production by:

- making more moisture available in a generally dry climate;
- improving the soil with fertile deposits of top soil and plant debris.

In 1981/82 a small project was set up under the French Volunteer Service (AFVP) in the Rissiam region, near Kongoussi. This project developed the technique of permeable rock dams. These became so popular that between 1982 and 1987, 148 permeable rock dams were built with the assistance of AFVP. The technical model of AFVP was the starting point for PATECORE's permeable rock dams.

PATECORE'S APPROACH AND OBJECTIVES

PATECORE began in 1988 with the aim of introducing an integrated, approach to conservation of village resources. This was to be achieved through discussion between villagers, project staff and other organisations working in the same village.

The Programme Allemand CILSS (the German Programme for the Sahelian Countries) had already successfully tested this type of approach in Burkina Faso.

Specific objectives were that:

- Land use planning should be carried out by villagers, according to their traditional methods of classifying land.

- Conservation structures – such as permeable rock dams – should be built as carefully as possible to reduce maintenance requirements.

- No techniques should be used which were too difficult for the people to construct and look after.

- Assistance by the project would be limited to
  – transport
  – technology development
  – training
  – support for the process of collaboration.

ACTIVITIES AND TECHNIQUES

We will look closely at one of PATECORE's main conservation activities – the technique of permeable rock dams.

PERMEABLE ROCK DAM

Burkina Faso

33

Permeable rock dams (PRD) are the most important conservation technique in the area, and the project views these as the "backbone" of its activities.

During the rainy season, large quantities of rainwater runoff are produced on the barren hillsides, where overgrazing has removed most of the vegetation. This runoff collects in small gullies and then flows down towards the valleys. This is no longer a gentle flow which spreads and waters the crops. These days it has become a torrent which cuts channels in the centre of the fertile valleys.

STARTING TO FILL A GULLY

Permeable rock dams help to control the runoff and stabilise the valleys. At the same time water is spread, and crop performance is improved.

PATECORE has taken the design developed by the nearby AFVP project and modified it to make the dams more durable and to reduce the amount of maintenance required. The permeable rock dams constructed under PATECORE are long, low dams made of loose stone, which stretch across valley floors, spreading floodwater and healing gullies. Usually the height of the dams is only 50 cm, but they can be up to 800 metres in length. Water doesn't stand behind the dam for long, because it filters through the loose stone wall.
(See technical section.)

PROJECT MANAGEMENT AND ORGANISATION OF WORK

Management of the Project:

PATECORE has up to ten local and expatriate staff at the project headquarters in Kongoussi. They see their role as facilitating development, rather than "managing" activities directly.

Coordination of Development Activities in the Province:

PATECORE has helped set up the Provincial Land Development Coordinating Committee. This committee is made up of government officials at the provincial level, and all the development agencies which are active in the province. The committee can plan activities in a coordinated way which will enable them to work out a common overall strategy for development in the area. By working in this way, they can ensure that there is no unnecessary duplication of activities, that they agree on technical solutions, that there is no "competition" between them, and that the villagers do not become confused because of different approaches and incentives.

Organisation of Work:

When a village requests assistance with planning and implementing conservation measures, this is what happens.

1. Village requests for assistance are screened by the Provincial Land Development Coordinating Committee (see above).

2. If approved, extension agents visit the village and discuss what must be done to overcome the problems the villagers face.

3. A Village Land Resource Management Committee is formed.

4. In cooperation with extension agents from various organisations, planning of the village land use takes place using aerial photographs. The villagers draw outlines on the aerial photographs of the different categories of their land which follow the traditional system of classification. This mixture of the traditional and the modern works well, and it does not take long to train villagers to interpret aerial photographs.

AERIAL PHOTOS ARE USED FOR LAND-USE PLANNING

5. A village land-use management plan is then drawn up by the Village Land Resource Management Committee. This plan outlines the improved management of each of the land categories, with a timetable for action.

6. Villagers are trained in techniques such as surveying with water-tube levels and siting of permeable rock dams. Guidance is also given on organisational aspects.

7. Some hand tools are supplied to the village committee.

8. The villagers stake out the alignment of the permeable rock dams in the field.

9. Stones and rocks are collected voluntarily on a group basis, and then transported, free of charge, by the project's lorries.

10. Construction is supervised by a project extensionist in the first year, then by a locally trained technician in the second year, and after that by the villagers themselves. Usually families carry out the construction on their own.

Incentives:

PATECORE has a very clear policy on incentives. It believes that the people should be given significant support in carrying out this type of activity and not have to rely entirely on their own resources.

For this reason PATECORE provides lorries free of charge to transport stone for the villagers. Availability of stone is of course the major problem with the construction of permeable rock dams. The argument in favour of the lorries is as follows:

1. Donkey carts are too slow to cope with the size and urgency of the problem ("erosion is faster than a donkey cart").

2. Lorries are only required in the construction stage, so no dependence on them will be created for other activities.

3. The people are so poor that they cannot be expected to contribute a significant amount to the running costs of the lorries.

However it is in this last respect that PATECORE differs most from the earlier established AFVP project. The belief of AFVP is that villagers should contribute a proportion (approximately a half) of the running cost for transport by lorries. AFVP believe that transport should eventually be taken over and managed by the village committees themselves.

In addition to the lorries, PATECORE supplies hand tools on a revolving-fund basis. Food-for-work is not used by PATECORE.

Participation

There is a clear division of work and responsibilities between the project and the people. In summary the people's participation is required in:

• the original request for assistance
• setting up village committees
• developing a village land-use management plan

35

- supplying volunteers for training
- contributing the labour, voluntarily, for all activities
- monitoring
- future planning and supervision of development activities.

The project concentrates on providing training, technological guidance and transport – as well as helping to coordinate development activities.

A TRAINING SESSION USING AERIAL PHOTOS

TRAINING AND EXTENSION

Training is one of PATECORE's main priorities. PATECORE trains villagers in planning the use of their land and in various conservation techniques.

Staff from government agencies and other projects are trained as well. This helps to ensure that techniques and approaches are the same for all the organisations in the area.

Training courses are held at the project headquarters near Kongoussi, where there are purpose-built classrooms.

YIELDS AND BENEFITS

Permeable rock dams improve crop yields very considerably – by between approximately 50% and 130%. Yields of sorghum can be increased to as high as 2,000 kg/ha. Because rich sediment builds up behind the dams each season, crop yields improve over the first few years.

A summary of the main benefits expected from permeable rock dams:

- harvesting and spreading of flood-waters for better crops
- a reduction in the speed and erosive force of runoff
- silting up of gullies with fertile deposits
- prevention of further erosion
- rehabilitation of abandoned land (in some cases)
- raising the water table.

Gombraogo Ouedragogo, a farmer whose land has been improved by a permeable rock dam.

"This area was so dry and degraded, I abandoned it for seven long years. I was farming elsewhere when I heard about the project. So I came back here last year and we built this dam. It has worked very well and I'm very happy with it."

PROBLEMS OUTSTANDING: WHERE NOW?

Limitations of Permeable Rock Dams

Permeable rock dams are a very effective technique, but their impact is limited. This is for two reasons.

36

1. Permeable rock dams use a large amount of stone and labour, and therefore only a small number can be built during one season.

2. Since they are particularly suited to valley bottoms, their main benefits are concentrated on those who live there rather than being spread among the whole community.

TECHNICAL PROBLEMS

PATECORE has developed the design of PRDs, but there are some technical problems which sometimes occur. These include:

• waterlogging on heavy soils
• siltation with sand rather than soil
• tunnelling of runoff below dams in some soils.

Lorries for Transport of Stone

The project considers that people are too poor to pay anything towards the cost of the lorries. However this makes it very difficult for other projects which believe that beneficiaries should contribute something.

Keeping up with Demand

The popularity of permeable rock dams is so great that it is difficult for PATECORE to keep up with demand! The project is trying to emphasise other techniques which are quicker and cheaper to implement.

LESSONS AND CONCLUSIONS

1. Coordination of development organisations working within the same area is extremely important. The establishment of the Provincial Coordinating Committee is a positive step towards achieving this in Bam Province.

2. The responsibility for overall planning and management of village resources has been given to the villagers themselves. Planning of land use by the village committees ensures that local priorities and development efforts are matched.

3. Requiring voluntary labour for construction of conservation works ensures that villagers are committed to what they do. Participation by the "beneficiaries" is essential for long-term development.

4. Using traditional systems of land classification together with aerial photographs is a mixture of the very old and the very new – but it has been shown to work effectively as a basis for planning.

5. Training of extension workers from Government departments and other projects leads to improved cooperation, and helps make sure that extension messages and techniques are similar.

6. The design of the permeable rock dam is based on systems tried originally by other projects – learning from others' experience where possible is always useful.

7. The question of mechanisation must be approached very carefully to ensure that dependence and expectations are not created. There is also the danger of projects having conflicting approaches.

8. Permeable rock dams are successful here, but this is a technique which can be used only in certain specific situations.

9. There is a need to develop cheaper techniques which can be applied more widely.

●KENYA●

Kenya is favoured by having high-altitude areas of good agricultural potential where most of the population lives. Nevertheless Kenya suffers occasional food shortages. One of the reasons for this is that over three quarters of the country is, in fact, arid or semi-arid. These areas are home to an increasing number of people as the country's population rises at about 4% per year – one of the fastest growth rates in Africa.

Agricultural production is threatened in many parts of the country by soil erosion. Soil conservation techniques for the highland areas are well developed and the conservation activities of self-help groups in Machakos District in eastern Kenya are particularly

effective. In the more arid areas, such as Turkana district in the far north-west, water harvesting is needed for dryland cropping to be possible. There are several projects testing systems of water harvesting, which is a new technique for Kenya.

We have taken one project from each of these two contrasting districts and looked at their different approaches to soil and water conservation. They are:

• the National Soil and Water Conservation Project in Machakos District
• the Lokitaung Pastoral Development Project, based at Lokitaung in Turkana District

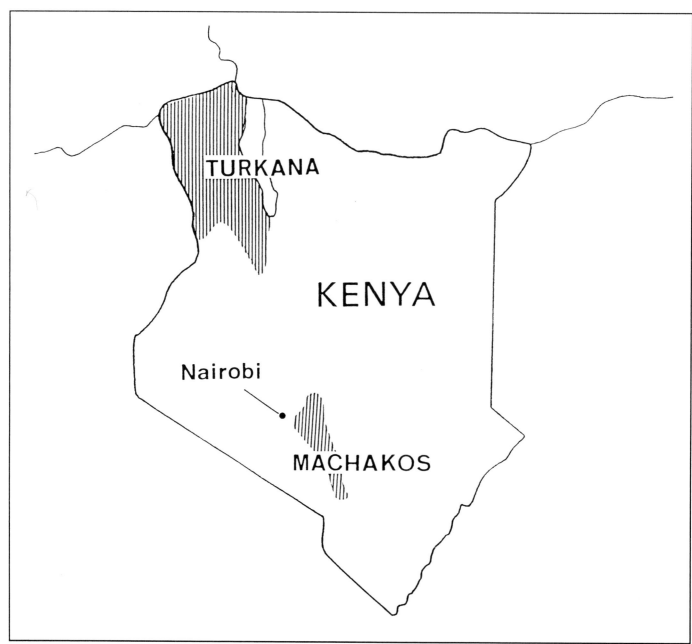

I. THE NATIONAL SOIL AND WATER CONSERVATION PROJECT – MACKAKOS DISTRICT

SUMMARY

Machakos has the reputation for being the District with the best soil and water conservation record in Kenya. Over 70% of the arable land has been terraced. However during colonial days there was strong resistance to soil conservation within Machakos. The change in attitude has been the result of campaigns and support from the National Soil and Water Conservation Project. Success has also depended on the strength of the groups which implement much of the conservation. The farmers, many of whom are women, have recognised the benefits of terracing.

Conservation of moisture and also soil has led to better and more reliable crop yields.

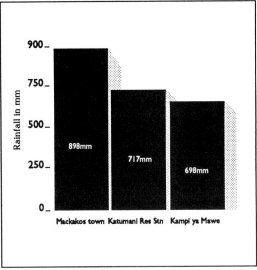

Annual Average Rainfall

> Name: National Soil and Water Conservation Project (Machakos District)
>
> Contact: The District Soil Conservation Officer, Machakos
>
> Address: The District Agricultural Office, Machakos, Kenya
>
> Status: Government Project
>
> Sponsor/Donor: Swedish International Development Agency (SIDA)
>
> Date of Start: 1974 project initiated; 1979 field work began in Machakos District; 1989 expanded to whole country

BACKGROUND

Machakos District in eastern Kenya has a large and growing population, which has to support itself on limited agricultural land. With an average of 72 people per square kilometre (census of 1979), most land which can be cropped is already in use. Much of the district has a marginal or semi-arid climate, and crop yields are commonly affected by lack of rainfall.

Machakos is hilly, and erosion has become increasingly widespread over the last twenty years as more land is cleared for cultivation. Much newly cultivated land is to be found on the hillsides, where erosion rates are higher. Pressure for more agricultural land has meant that livestock are steadily being squeezed on to smaller and smaller areas of land, which are then overgrazed and more prone to erosion.

Over most of the District, families depend on home-grown food for their daily diet. Maize has become the most popular cereal during this century, replacing the more drought-resistant crops of sorghum and millet. Though the average rainfall figures for Machakos are quite high, there are regular periods of drought during the rainfall seasons. Lack of adequate rainfall for maize, and an ever decreasing supply of productive land has made the farmers appreciate the need for soil and water conservation.

39

Soil conservation was first introduced to the District by the colonial government in the 1940s. Some of the techniques developed during this period were effective, but the fact that they were based on enforced communal work meant that soil conservation was bitterly resented by the people, and it developed a bad name.

Little happened immediately after Independence in 1963, until a new soil and water conservation campaign began in the 1970s. This campaign started up just at the time when the people were becoming increasingly concerned about the future of their farm land. People were now anxious to listen to advice, and were ready to participate in conservation activities.

In summary:

- Slopes are steep in Machakos, and erosion rates high.
- Erosion is getting worse due to the expanding cropped area.
- Drought spells regularly affect yields, especially of maize.
- Enforced conservation in colonial times didn't work.
- By the 1970s people were ready to respond to a new campaign.

NSWCP'S APPROACH AND OBJECTIVES

The National Soil and Water Conservation Project (NSWCP), supported by the Swedish International Development Agency (SIDA), began in 1974. Machakos was chosen to be a pilot district, and a full soil and water conservation campaign was launched there in 1979. This became a national campaign with support from local government as well as the Ministry of Agriculture.

The overall objective of NSWCP is:

"to contribute to food security and to raise the standard of living of the rural population – through suitable conservation practices."

In the early days, some of the work was paid, but the policy quickly became one of voluntary participation, supported by:
- technical advice
- tools.

Machakos was an excellent choice of district to begin operations. This was because:

1. Erosion was a serious problem, and as we have seen, the people themselves were concerned about the effect on their crop yields.

2. A suitable soil and water conservation technique – *fanya-juu* terracing – was already well established in the district.

3. Strong and active self-help *mwethya* groups already existed and they were ready and willing to work on conservation projects.

ACTIVITIES AND TECHNIQUES

"Fanya-juu" terracing

The focus of the soil and water conservation project has been on improving arable land. It is in the cropped fields where erosion has had the most damaging effect on productivity and farmers' income.

MWETHYA GROUP CREATING FANYA-JUU TERRACES

The basis of the system is the development of bench terraces over a period of time. The main technique used is *fanya-juu* terracing. This means, in Kiswahili, "do-up" and it refers to the way that soil is thrown up the slope from a ditch to form an earth embankment or bund. Several of these terrace banks are made across a field, on the contour, and over time the land between the bunds levels off. The field then develops the characteristic "steps" of bench terraces (see technical section). Soil and rainwater are conserved between the *fanya-juu* bunds.

40

The technical objective is two-fold:
• to keep rainfall where it falls;
• to keep soil in the field.

The end result is better growing conditions for the crop, both immediately, because of an increase in the amount of moisture available, and in the long term, because the soil is conserved.

Each farm is surveyed to see whether it requires a cutoff drain to protect it from surplus rainfall runoff. The cutoff drain is usually designed to hold all the runoff which flows into it, and therefore it is sometimes known as an "infiltration ditch".

The alignment of the terraces is surveyed along the contour using a simple line level. The spacing between the terraces depends on the slope of the land. (For details see technical section.)

Since the mid-1980s the District has achieved an average of 1,000 kilometres of new *fanya-juu* terraces constructed each year, as well as several hundred kilometres of cutoff drains. The campaign has been so effective that it is estimated that 70% of all the cultivated land has now been terraced. From a hillside above Machakos town it is easy to believe these figures! The remaining unterraced plots are mainly in the lower, drier areas.

70% OF ALL CULTIVATED LAND HAS NOW BEEN TERRACED

Terracing is not the only technical component of the project in Machakos. Also recommended and used, though on a smaller scale, are:
• grass strips along the contour
• contour ploughing
• simple gully control measures
• tree planting
• protection of riverbanks
• grazing control

"DEVELOPED" TERRACES WITH FODDER GRASSES
PLANTED ON THE BANK TO HOLD THE SOIL IN PLACE.

Fodder grasses can be planted on the top of the terrace bank to hold the earth together. The farmer benefits from this source of valuable cattle feed, and land which might otherwise be wasted is put to good use. Likewise, the trenches are often used for growing bananas, which do well because of the extra water which collects there.

Fanya-juu terracing uses a considerable amount of labour but it is well understood by the people in eastern Kenya, and has been proved to be effective.

PROJECT MANAGEMENT AND ORGANISATION OF WORK

Management of the Project:

NSWCP falls under the Ministry of Agriculture's Soil and Water Conservation Branch. In Machakos it is supervised by the District Soil Conservation Officer. Representatives of local farmers participate in planning through the District Agricultural Committee.

Kenya

41

Organisation of Conservation Work:

The Ministry of Agriculture in Machakos holds soil conservation campaigns each year, but everyday conservation activities are organised and carried out by the people themselves.

Soil conservation work is normally undertaken by self-help *mwethya* groups. A group decides which member's land is to be terraced on which day, and then the members meet and work collectively.

Some individuals, who are wage earners, sometimes decide to employ people to carry out the work for them since family labour on its own is not enough.

Incentives:

Farmers are not paid for any soil conservation work on their own land in Machakos.

HAND TOOLS WAITING FOR DISTRIBUTION

Some incentives however are given to assist them with the work. This help is in the form of hand tools, which wear out very quickly in the hard soils of the District. During 1988 over 4,000 tools were distributed for soil conservation work – these included shovels, hoes, pangas (machetes), mattocks, pickaxes, crowbars and wheelbarrows.

Tools are allocated according to availability, and the demand for tools is far greater than the number available. Most of the conservation work is done with the farmer's own tools.

Participation:

The people of Machakos participate fully in the whole conservation programme. This participation is largely through the self-help *mwethya* groups. *Mwethya* groups are traditional in the area, though nowadays the majority are registered with the Ministry of Culture and Social Services. There are over 3,000 registered groups in Machakos District, with group membership ranging between 20 and 150. The vast majority of the members are women.

These well organised groups count soil conservation as one of their main activities. *Mwethya* groups have been the backbone of the soil conservation success story in Machakos. The sight of a hundred or so people digging a terrace together and singing at the same time is impressive!

KYUNGU MWETHYA GROUP MEETING

The Kyungu Mwethya Group is active in an area some 5 kilometres to the south of Machakos town. There are 78 members of this group, which was founded in 1986. All the members are women. Very few are unmarried or younger than 25 years old. Some of their menfolk are away in Machakos or Nairobi earning wages, others are unemployed.

The chairperson, Munyira Maleve, explains how the membership fee is KSh 100 (about $5) and if anyone misses the weekly afternoon work-meeting on Wednesdays they pay a fine of KSh10. The funds raised are used for a variety of purposes, including buying tools.

Each week the group meets on some-one's farm to carry out soil conserva-tion work or other related activities. Each member is given a fixed amount of work to do. For digging a *fanya-juu* terrace this is normally "two shovels length" of terracing. Each member brings her own tools. Group tools used to be shared, but that didn't prove a good system, as the tools were not looked after well. Now they are allocated to individuals.

By 1990 each member has had at least a portion of her farm terraced. This group also has a communal one-acre plot of onions and beans. Other groups in the area undertake income-generating activities such as shop-keeping, operating maize mills, or poultry keeping.

Munyira Maleve tells how the *mwethya* group acts as a kind of insurance – helping out when a mem-ber falls sick. The group can decide to allocate one of its work days to planting, weeding or harvesting a member's plot for example. No won-der most married women in Machakos are members of *mwethya* groups!

TRAINING AND EXTENSION

Extension work is carried out in the same way as for crop and animal pro-duction. The Ministry of Agriculture has a well-organised system of advising farmers called the "training and visit" system. This consists of regular visits by extension agents to "contact farmers", carrying specific recommendations each time. The contact farmers then relay the recommendations to the rest of the com-munity. Although the system is rather inflexible, it generally works well.

Before delivering messages, the Ministry's extension staff are trained through a system of monthly work-shops. These workshops cover all aspects of agricultural production, and concentrate on soil conservation during certain periods of the year – for example after crops have been harvested in January. The soil and water conserva-tion programme fits neatly into the extension workers' calendar. The main seasonal campaign takes place after the crops have been harvested, when there are no other "crop production mes-sages" to give out.

In Machakos District the contact farmers for extension visits are groups rather than individuals since self-help groups in Machakos meet on a regular basis.

YIELDS AND BENEFITS

The main reason that terracing has been so successful in Machakos is the effect it has had on crop yields. Farmers can clearly see that terraced land produces better crops year after year than neglected land. The reasons for this are many, but the most important one is that rainfall is kept where it falls.

Only a few detailed studies have been carried out to measure the effect of ter-racing on crop yields in Machakos, but a recent report shows that on average ter-raced fields yield 400kg more maize per hectare than unterraced ones. This is an increase of 50% or more.

There are other important benefits of terracing:

• Where a whole catchment area has been conserved, there is an improve-ment in stream flow – very important for village water supply.
• Terracing is sometimes viewed as a "proof of occupancy" or a claim of ownership.
• Some farmers take great pride in the appearance of a well-terraced "sham-

ba" (farm) and this leads to an overall improvement in the standard of farming.

Not everyone, however, has benefited, and there is still a significant proportion of crop land unterraced. There are a number of very poor, female-headed households where the women cannot find the time or the money to join in *mwethya* activities. Their land will remain prone to erosion and the poor crop yields which result.

PROBLEMS OUTSTANDING: WHERE NOW?

ERODED GRAZING LAND

Erosion of Grazing Land:
Although most of the cropped land is well conserved, there is a serious problem with erosion of grazing land. An appropriate approach to this problem needs to be developed.

Alternative Techniques:
Fanya-juu terracing is costly in terms of the considerable labour it requires. The project recognises this and has recently begun to work with cheaper alternatives such as vegetative strips and agro-

forestry techniques. In drier areas, some sort of water harvesting system would be more appropriate.

Vegetation of Terrace Banks:
The Ministry recommends that terrace banks should be planted with fodder species, such as bana grass. So far this has been poorly adopted by farmers, with the result that the banks are prone to erosion. Part of the problem is an inadequate supply of planting material and a lack of transport.

Shortage of Tools:
There is a shortage of hand tools in Machakos. Tools wear out quickly in the hard soil, and some groups are hindered by a lack of implements to work with.

Monitoring:
Although this is one of the best examples of soil conservation in sub-Saharan Africa, there is little information on the effect of conservation on crop yields or farm incomes. The project accepts that monitoring needs to be improved.

The Poorest Households:
The poorest households, which are often headed by women, frequently miss out on the benefits of soil conservation. A way of assisting poorer households in the community needs to be found.

Other Districts:
Machakos and neighbouring Kitui have an especially good record for soil conservation. But the programme has not yet been as effective elsewhere in Kenya. Where self-help groups are not part of the local tradition, and where returns from conservation are not so immediate, the techniques and approach need to be modified.

LESSONS AND CONCLUSIONS

1. Machakos has a serious problem of soil erosion because of the steep slopes and the expanding area under cultivation.

2. Terracing in Machakos is popular due largely to the rapid benefits it gives in terms of improved crop performance.

3. The existence of well developed self-help groups is one of the main reasons for the success of conservation activi-

ties in Machakos. Elsewhere experience has shown that it is very difficult to form effective groups if they do not already exist.

4. The conservation technique used is not new to the area. It is technically sound, and because people have had experience of it for a number of years they accept it more readily. New ideas are much more difficult to introduce.

5. In Machakos, where the level of participation from the people is good, the most important support on offer from NSWCP is in the form of technical guidance and tools, which are an effective and suitable incentive.

6. The project has benefited from being integrated into the Ministry of Agriculture's well-established extension system.

7. Another factor in the success of the programme in Machakos has been the well-publicised campaigns for conservation.

8. Machakos is an example of a site-specific success story where a combination of factors has created favourable conditions for the programme. Reproducing the results in districts where conditions differ is not proving easy.

9. There are still problems to overcome. These include the lack of an effective conservation approach for the grazing

Mukethe Mbithi is a member of the Kyungu Mwethya group.

"Before making the terraces we didn't have good harvests because the soil was eroded. When we put fertilizer on, the water washed it into the river and the maize grew short. But when we made terraces the soil erosion stopped and we got good crops."

areas, the need for suitable techniques in the driest zones, and the difficulty of involving the poorest households in community conservation activities.

Kenya

45

2. LOKITAUNG PASTORAL DEVELOPMENT PROJECT – TURKANA DISTRICT

SUMMARY

The Lokitaung Pastoral Development Project in Turkana District helps semi-nomadic Turkana people. LPDP is working in an arid and difficult region where there is a history of hardship and relief food aid. The programme began as the

"Turkana Water Harvesting Project", helping to develop systems of water harvesting for crop production, while also introducing animal ploughing. The project has trained local people – many of them women – to become water harvesting technicians. The most interesting aspect of the project is its evolution into a long-term development programme, mostly concerned with pastoral production – the main occupation of the local people. LPDP is largely managed by the local people themselves. In the context of the problems faced, LPDP has made significant progress.

BACKGROUND

The vast majority of the Turkana people in Kenya's arid north-west are pastoralists. They herd camels, cattle, sheep and goats. The climate of Turkana is hot and dry, and when the rains do come, they are short and unreliable. The average rainfall is 360mm, with as little as 115mm in some years, and as much as 650mm in others. Pastoralism is the most viable subsistence system. The balance can, however, be upset by disease or drought. Crop production is not possible without irrigation or some form of water harvesting. In some areas, the Turkana carry out a little sorghum cropping, especially where flooding of rivers leaves some moisture in the ground.

Name: Lokitaung Pastoral Development Project

Contact: Pius Chuchu, Project Secretary

Address: P.O. Lokitaung, via Lodwar, Turkana District

Status: Self-help Project

Sponsor/ Donor: Oxfam (Oxford, UK) supported by the Intermediate Technology Development Group (Rugby, UK)

Date of Start:
• 1984 started as the Turkana Water Harvesting Project
• 1990 became the Lokitaung Pastoral Development project

TURKANA WITH LIVESTOCK

Development projects have rarely succeeded in Turkana. Often projects have been based on food relief, and have been introduced hurriedly without proper planning. When the need for food relief ends, the "development" process also stops. Irrigation and fishery schemes have both been tried in Turkana, but with little success. In most of these cases the technology was inappropriate, and the social issues not properly considered.

Turkana District has always suffered from natural hardships – in 1979/80 livestock deaths and food shortages led to severe hunger, and the creation of relief camps. Food-for-work schemes were based around these camps, and one of the activities under this programme was water harvesting. The aim was to construct earth bunds to "harvest" rainwater runoff for growing crops and fodder. But most of the structures were poorly designed, and no thought was given to how the community would use the water harvesting systems afterwards. The people were more interested in the food than the activity! The result was that most of the structures were abandoned after being built.

LPDP'S APPROACH AND OBJECTIVES

The Lokitaung Pastoral Development Project began in 1984 as the "Turkana Water Harvesting Project" with the two objectives of:

- demonstrating appropriate rainwater harvesting systems;
- introducing animal draught for ploughing and earth moving.

This was at a time when food-for-work was still widely used by projects in Turkana. LPDP had little choice but to use food-for-work also, for the construction of rainwater harvesting systems. However the aim was to reduce food rations gradually and to put the people in charge of food distribution.

It was decided to organise management of the

project under a local Management Board drawn from members of committees in each of the three project centres. The committees themselves would be based on existing local institutions. Management would be by the people themselves – with a minimum of outside help.

Activities at the start were centred around improved rainwater harvesting for sorghum production. The idea was that crops would help to supplement income from livestock, and by bartering surplus grain, families could rebuild their herds. The policy was to help families who only had a few animals remaining to "get back on their feet" as pastoralists.

Rainwater harvesting can make sorghum production a little more reliable in this area – and it was believed that improvement could be made to some of the bunding techniques used by earlier relief programmes. There was also much traditional agricultural knowledge to build on – an excellent starting point!

ACTIVITIES AND TECHNIQUES

Water harvesting:

LPDP helps to improve existing sorghum gardens, and to establish some new ones. Traditionally some Turkana plant sorghum where rainwater runoff accumulates in natural depressions

Kenya

WATER HARVESTING BUND BEING CONSTRUCTED

47

making growing conditions favourable. The local sorghum variety requires very little water and can be harvested after two months. LPDP aimed to improve the collection of rainwater runoff to give the crop more moisture to survive the arid conditions.

LPDP had a number of problems with early design of water harvesting systems. However much was learnt from the experiences of other projects in the area. The technique has been developed over the years, and the locally trained technicians have helped to design improvements – such as a new spillway system, locally called "Irimeto" (see technical section).

The rainwater harvesting system consists of earth bunds on three sides of individual plots. These plots range in size from half an hectare to two hectares. The plots are sited where small channels bring runoff during storms –and the runoff is held by the earth bunds. Surplus runoff runs away around the tips of the two "arms" which extend up the slope.

The earth bunds are built to a maximum of a metre in height, and are up to eight metres in base width. Although the earth is carried in metal basins by the workers, oxen have been trained to pull a scoop to bring heaps of soil closer. The scoops are also used to level the plots, so that the water will spread better, and the crops grow more evenly.

Animal Draught:

LOCALLY MADE PLOUGH

In addition to introducing oxen scoops, LPDP has trained oxen and donkeys to plough. Traditionally land is prepared by hand. The project brought in an animal draught trainer from another part of Kenya, who in turn trained one local Turkana in each of the three centres. A new and appropriate type of plough has been introduced – based on the Ethiopian *ard*. The ploughshares are made by local blacksmiths, and the frames of the ploughs are made from local wood.

Activities at the Community Stores:

Each of the three project centres has a community store which operates with a revolving fund. The two main activities are:
- Trading of skins (of sheep and goats). Families deliver skins to the stores.

ANIMAL DRAUGHT IS USED FOR PLOUGHING AND EARTH MOVING

These are bought at a fair price and then sold to a mobile trader.
- Sales of food grain to assist food security. Each store keeps a supply of grain for sale. This guards against shortages in food supply.

FAMILIES DELIVER SKINS TO THE COMMUNITY STORE

PROJECT MANAGEMENT AND ORGANISATION OF WORK

Management of the Project:

LPDP is managed by a local Management Board. Members of the Management Board are drawn from the local committees, which are based at the three centres of activity – Loarengak, Kachoda and Kaaling. These three committees are based on traditional institutions.

LPDP receives financial and technical support from OXFAM and the Intermediate Technology Development Group respectively. A small number of local project staff are employed, including the Project Secretary, and the following staff at each of the three centres:

- an elder ("Ekarabon")
- a monitoring/ store person
- a water harvesting technician
- an animal draught trainer.

Several of the project staff are women, as are the majority of the members of the local committees.

Organisation of the Water Harvesting Work:

When assistance is requested by a land user, the process is as follows:

1. The plot is visited by the local water harvesting technician, who recommends the work to be done if:

- the site is suitable
- the applicant has at least 15 sheep/ goats
- a workforce can be organised
- the family has traditional land rights.

2. If approved, the technician designs the structures in cooperation with the land user.

3. A food-for-work contract is drawn up. This states how many bags of grain will be given to the family when the work is finished. In early 1989, this averaged 6 sacks (90kg each) per plot.

4. The work force is organised by the land user, and is usually composed of family members and friends. An oxen scoop may be borrowed from the local committee, but most of the construction is carried out by hand with simple tools such as hoes and basins.

5. The land user then contributes a goat to the village committee to build up community funds.

The contract system has worked very well, and very few families have failed to complete work on their gardens.

Incentives:

Food-for-work has been the main incentive to assist families in construction of water harvesting systems. There is a long history of food-for-work in the area, and when the project began, it would not have been possible to start such a programme without some food aid. The project has a clear policy on food-for-work:

1. to use food aid only when necessary, and to reduce rations gradually – thereby reducing dependence.

2. to put the people in charge of the distribution of their food.

One of the first moves by the project was to put elders in charge of the distri-

Kenya

49

bution of food rations. This delegated responsibility to the local people. A steady reduction in food rations has been achieved, and by 1989, the ration had been reduced to a quarter of that first given out.

Participation:

One of the most positive aspects of the project is the way it has achieved local participation in management and the organisation of activities.

Voluntary participation in construction of water harvesting systems is growing all the time. In 1990 there was a shortage of food-for-work supplies, and yet construction continued. Maintenance of structures, almost everywhere, is voluntary.

TRAINING

PEOPLE ARE TRAINED TO USE A "LINE LEVEL" FOR SURVEYING

There are regular training courses when staff are trained in a variety of skills. These include:

- water harvesting technology – design of systems;
- animal draught – how to use oxen to plough and scoop earth;
- monitoring – recording of data such as work rates and yields;
- general leadership and management skills.

YIELDS AND BENEFITS

CREDIT: Olivia Graham/OXFAM

AN IMPROVED SORGHUM GARDEN

By June 1990 over 200 families had received assistance to improve their sorghum plots. There are no exact figures on yield improvements, but the people say that yields have increased. More importantly the harvest is more reliable. It is said that a good harvest can be expected about three years out of five.

YIELDS HAVE INCREASED AND THE HARVEST IS MORE RELIABLE

50

PROBLEMS OUTSTANDING: WHERE NOW?

Change in Emphasis:

There are limits to what water harvesting for crop production can do for the Turkana. Many of the families in the area have already improved their plots. The Management Board has now decided to change the emphasis of the project from water harvesting to include livestock and food security.

Outside Assistance:

The project hopes to become self-reliant in the future. Already food-for-work is being phased out. But it remains to be seen how truly independent of outside assistance the project can become.

Costs:

The water harvesting system is quite expensive – especially in relation to the unreliable yields in the arid conditions of Turkana. However costs have been reduced by the use of the oxen scoops. There may be a possibility of developing new ideas, such as using brushwood or planted shrubs to catch wind-blown sand and form bunds in a "natural" way.

Animal Draught:

Oxen/donkey ploughing has not been adopted as quickly as was hoped – it takes time to train people and their animals. However ploughing has been made quicker and easier now with the introduction of the Ethiopian *ard*-type plough.

Crop Husbandry:

Crop husbandry could be improved. This is one of the objectives of the future programme. A wider variety of crops and varieties could be planted, better pest control introduced, and more use made of "take-a-chance" planting of crops like cowpeas.

Monitoring:

Improved monitoring systems are needed. These are indeed being developed in order to measure yields, the rate of restocking which has taken place, and other important effects of the project.

LESSONS AND CONCLUSIONS

1. LPDP has been successful, despite its limited achievements, in the context of the very difficult environment of northwest Turkana.

2. The project has managed to develop into a community-based programme, with a reduced dependence on support from outside.

3. The project has also evolved from a simple water harvesting project to a long-term programme focusing particularly on the people's main priority, pastoralism.

4. Existing local institutions have made a very good base for the development of local management committees.

5. Food-for-work often leads to poor development projects, which do not last after the food relief ends. LPDP has managed to reduce the amounts of food allocated, and put its distribution into the hands of local people. The project is well on the way to phasing the food out of its programme.

6. Training of local people in the technical skills of water harvesting and animal draught has worked well.

7. The water harvesting system used by the project, although quite costly, works well. LPDP has taken models from other projects, and used its own experience to develop a system over a period of time. Locally trained staff have made an important contribution in this process.

8. Problems which are being faced by LPDP include the relatively high cost of its water harvesting system, the need to improve monitoring, a variable standard of crop husbandry and a rather uncertain future.

Kenya

51

● MALI ●

Much of northern Mali is arid and barren, land where only pastoralists can make a living. Although the population of Mali is quite low overall, the majority of the people are concentrated in the wetter south, where the agricultural land is becoming scarce.

There is land degradation in parts of the arid north, and this has been made worse by the droughts of recent years. There is erosion also in southern Mali, with its higher rainfall and better land. Cotton is the most important cash crop in the south.

There are some very interesting traditional techniques of conservation in Mali – which are not widely known about. However Mali has not had much experience of soil conservation programmes and it is only in the last few years that a significant number of projects have started up.

First, we visit an area where there is a wide range of conservation techniques, all entirely traditional – the Dogon Plateau.

Second, we look at one of the longest established soil conservation projects, situated in the cotton growing zone of southern Mali – the "Projet Lutte Anti-Erosive" (Anti-Erosion Project) of the "Compagnie Malienne de Developpement des Textiles" (Malian Textile Development Company).

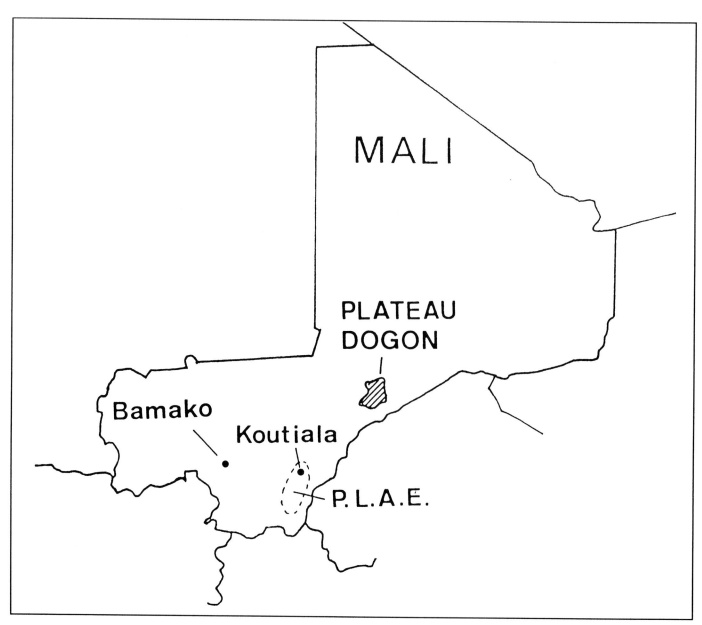

1. TRADITIONAL SOIL AND WATER CONSERVATION ON THE DOGON PLATEAU

INTRODUCTION

The Dogon Plateau is home to a wide variety of traditional soil and water conservation measures. There can be few other areas in sub-Saharan Africa where the local people have devised such a range of conservation techniques including hillside terracing, stone lines, earth basins, planting pits and earth mounds. These traditional methods of conservation have been developed mainly to cope with the acute shortage of soil – and rain – on the plateau. Some of the techniques could be improved, and the people urgently need support to reduce erosion further. Nevertheless the main lesson from the Dogon Plateau is that there is much to learn from traditional ways of doing things which have often been ignored. Soil and water conservation projects should always begin by looking at what the people are doing for themselves.

BACKGROUND

WOMEN AT WORK IN DOGON VILLAGE

Situated in the eastern part of central Mali, the Dogon Plateau is well known to outsiders for its picturesque villages and spectacular cliffs and escarpments. The plateau is hilly and covered with rocky outcrops. But for the agricultural Dogon, the shortage of land to cultivate has always been a problem. Less than a quarter of the plateau's surface can be planted with crops, and much of the soil is just a thin cover over the rock.

The population density of about 25 people/ km2 is very high for an area with such little soil and such low rainfall. Strangely, the population is most concentrated on the rocky hillsides where there is the least cultivable land! In common with several other regions in Africa, one of the reasons that the people originally moved to the escarpments, was for security from raiders. Many families have chosen to stay there.

The large population simply cannot feed itself in times of drought. In low rainfall years many young men go to the towns and the better agricultural areas in search of seasonal work. Some families have even migrated from the area, settling in the south of Mali where there is better soil and more reliable rainfall.

The Dogon plateau is a low rainfall area and lack of rainfall has become an even more severe problem over the last 20 years. The annual average rainfall has diminished from 555mm to as little as 465mm during this period. Not only have crop yields suffered, but drinking water has become more scarce. Streams dry up earlier in the season, and the water tables have gradually fallen – which means that wells and boreholes have to be dug ever deeper and deeper.

As well as being low, the overall rainfall is also unreliable and individual rainstorms can be very intense. Naturally there is considerable runoff from the rocky surfaces. This leads to erosion of soil on the fields below – if the land is not well protected by soil conservation measures. Wind erosion is also a serious problem here during the dry season.

Much of the erosion caused by rainfall occurs on land which is too rocky to be cultivated. This is grazing land, and erosion here means that less vegetation grows for the cattle, sheep and goats. At the same time, money which is sent back to the villages by those working away is often used to buy livestock...and the problem of the grazing lands increases.

Mali

53

The Dogon however depend principally on their subsistence food crops. Most of the land cultivated is planted with sorghum and millet. Groundnuts are also common. In addition to rainfed farming, irrigated vegetable production is important close to the watercourses. The most common vegetable here is onions.

In summary, the problems on the Dogon Plateau are:

- a shortage of land to cultivate and thin soils
- a high population density
- low rainfall which has diminished over the last 20 years
- high rates of rainfall runoff from stony surfaces
- high rates of erosion – both by water and by wind
- overgrazing by livestock.

Because of their historical dependence on their food crops, the Dogon have simply had to develop methods to conserve their soil and water! Without these, they could not have survived.

ACTIVITIES AND TECHNIQUES

STONE LINES ARE BUILT WHERE LAND IS FLATTER

The Dogon have developed many different ways of conserving soil and water. Most are used in particular situations. For example hillside terracing is used only on the stony slopes, whereas stone lines are built where the land is flatter. Some techniques can be used in combination. For example earth mounding, which is very common, is often combined with stone lines or stone bunds.

Each of the main measures is described below. Details of sizes and specifications are given in the technical section of this book.

Hillside terraces

SOIL TAKEN FROM THE RIVER BED IS ADDED TO THE HILLSIDE TERRACES.

The hillside terraces of the Dogon consist of small stone walls which hold pockets of earth in place. Where there is quite a good supply of soil, the terraces may be more or less continuous along the hillside. Elsewhere they may be scattered, with individual terraces constructed between stone outcrops. Soil is normally levelled by hand within each terrace. Where the earth is not deep enough, extra soil may be added from nearby. Some terraces are built on bare rock – and all the soil is brought from outside ! (See the section on onion gardens below.)

This technique now less important than it was for three reasons.

1. People are gradually moving down from the hillsides now that there is no longer a security problem.

2. Construction and maintenance use a great deal of labour.

3. Recently, the lack of rainfall on the shallow soil has resulted in poor crops within the terraces.

Stone lines

Throughout the flatter areas of cultivation, wherever there is any loose stone, the Dogon construct stone lines. These lines are placed across the slope, in order to slow runoff and reduce erosion. Often the lines are just a string of individual stones – resembling crocodiles' teeth!.

These lines could be improved. The stones could be placed more carefully to avoid small rills forming between them, and the lines would be more effective if they followed the contour.

Stone bunds

These are larger structures than the stone lines, and less common. More labour is involved. They are preferred to stone lines where the land is more sloping, where erosion is worse and where there is a good supply of stone. As with stone lines, these bunds are built across the slope, and the idea is again to slow runoff and reduce erosion. But again they would be more effective if they were built more carefully, and if they followed the contour.

Earth Mounds

The technique of making small earth mounds between plants while weeding is very widespread on the Dogon plateau. These mounds are seen elsewhere in Mali. It is possible that the technique has only been adopted by the Dogon in the last half century. It is certainly growing in importance now.

When the young cereal crop is first weeded in July, the weeds are scraped together and covered by earth in the form of mounds between the plants. Each mound is about 20-30cm high. The mounds last throughout the season and have two useful effects. First they tend to slow down runoff as it flows through the field. Secondly the mounds act as "mini-compost heaps", and help maintain soil fertility.

Earth Basins

Some Dogon make small earth basins in places where the soil is deeper. The idea is to catch and hold every drop of rainwater where it falls – and of course this stops soil being lost also. This is one of the most effective techniques of all but it is quite labour intensive.

Each basin (of between one and four square metres) is made by building an

EARTH BASINS.

earth ridge in the form of a square. Construction takes place in the dry season, before planting. The ridges are built-up during weeding.

Planting Pits

As with earth mounds, this is a technique which is also found outside the

Boukary Yebeize

"When we make the basins and pits the water which would have left the field stays put, and so in the dry weather there is less crop damage. The yield is now higher. When we have enough rain the crops ripen well. By harvest time when we haven't used the techniques the millet can dry out, but everywhere we do use the techniques, the millet stays green".

55

Dogon plateau – even as far away as Yatenga in Burkina Faso where it is known as *zai*. Planting pits are quite small – only 15-20cm deep and 30cm or so in diameter. These pits are dug about a metre apart. Manure is added, and then several cereal seeds are sown into the centre of each pit.

The benefits are a concentration of rainfall around the plant roots, and a concentration of the effect of the manure/compost.

Planting pits can be used together with most other techniques. This is a popular technique although it is not as widespread as earth mounds.

Trash Lines

One measure which is becoming less commonly used is trash lines. These are narrow strips, made from cereal stems or even cut bush, which are aligned across the slope. They have the effect of slowing and filtering runoff and soil fertility is built up when the vegetative material decomposes. However, the problems are that the trash can easily be blown away before the rains come and cutting of foliage has recently been made illegal.

Onion gardens made with "transported earth"

The Dogon have an extraordinary tradition of creating onion gardens on bare rock! This is not a conservation measure in the same sense as the techniques already described, but it does show the skill with which the Dogon manage the little soil and water that they have.

Market gardening has been practiced for a long time on the Dogon plateau. Vegetables, and particularly onions, are grown close to seasonal watercourses, from which they are irrigated. However there is not enough land on the riverbanks, and in some areas there is bare rock on both sides of the watercourses. It is precisely here that the Dogon create new land for cultivation.

The "transported earth gardens" are started by building a network of small stone squares on the rock surface. Each square has sides of about one or one and a half metres. Silt is then dug from the riverbed, or earth collected from

TRANSPORTED EARTH GARDENS BEING CREATED

cracks in the rock nearby, and carried to the site. The squares are filled to an initial depth of about 15-20cm. Manure or compost is added to improve the fertility of the transported earth.

Vegetables are planted in these gardens during the dry season. Regular and careful watering is then carried out, by hand, from the riverbed. Onions mature quickly in the shallow soil. After harvesting the bulbs are crushed into pulp, squeezed into balls, and dried on the bare rock close to the gardens, ready for marketing.

ONIONS ARE PULPED AND SQUEEZED INTO BALLS FOR MARKETING

ORGANISATION OF WORK

Dogon society is still strongly traditional in all aspects, including agriculture and soil and water conservation. Agricultural land is divided into common fields, family fields and small plots belonging to the women. The main fields are used for sorghum and millet, but the women prefer to grow groundnuts, voandzeia ("Bambara groundnuts"), and various vegetables on their plots.

For most cropping activities the women join the men in the fields after they have prepared the midday meal. However women are traditionally not involved in building soil and water conservation structures except in the construction of onion gardens when they carry soil.

There is no strong tradition of group labour in soil conservation on the Dogon plateau. Normally the male members of the household work alone, though in some cases friends and neighbours may join together in informal working groups.

However a new agricultural development project on the plateau – the "Projet Vulgarisation Agricole" is attempting to involve village groups, which include young women, in soil conservation activities. The idea is that village working groups can speed up construction on an individual's field. Some payments are made to the groups for their labour.

YIELDS AND BENEFITS

There are no figures available for the benefits of the various techniques, either in terms of improved plant performance, or soil conserved. There is simply not enough known about the traditional systems of conservation. But what is certain is that the Dogon could not have continued as agriculturalists without these systems and would not continue to use them if they didn't think it was worthwhile, given the huge amount of labour which they take.

PROBLEMS OUTSTANDING: WHERE NOW?

The future of cropping on the Dogon plateau

Despite all the techniques which are used by the Dogon, erosion is still a

The Projet Vulgarisation Agricole, (PVA) which is an agricultural extension project, was set up at Bandiagara in the mid-1980s to help improve agriculture on the Dogon Plateau. PVA has a small soil conservation unit, and has recently begun to give technical assistance to the Dogon. The project has concentrated initially on improved designs for stone bunds. Training courses have been held, during which the use of the "A" frame – a simple surveying instrument to lay out contours – has been taught.

menace on the plateau. Overpopulation has lead to over-use of the land. The amount of cultivable land is growing smaller each year, and families are having to migrate. Help is urgently required to improve the conservation techniques, and to assist the people to carry out the work.

Improving the technology

The stone lines and stone bunds are the techniques which are in most need of improvement. Better placement of stone, the introduction of a foundation trench, and alignment on the contour are all improvements which PVA is trying to introduce. But this is only a first step – there is a great deal to do, and the work is urgent.

Tool supply

The Dogon are desperately short of appropriate hand tools to work with. This again is an area where some projects have begun to help.

Mali

57

LESSONS AND CONCLUSIONS

1. The Dogon plateau has a rich variety of soil and water conservation techniques which have been developed by the local people and implemented without outside assistance.

2. The combination of limited land, low rainfall and a growing population have forced people to look after their land. Without conservation of soil and water, cultivation could not have continued.

3. There is very little knowledge about the traditional techniques here – and there is much to be learnt. This is also true of other parts of sub-Saharan Africa. Such systems are usually ignored by soil conservation "experts".

4. Several of the measures could be applied in other parts of sub-Saharan Africa although most of them cannot be used in places where animal traction is used.

5. After careful study, these traditional techniques should be used as the starting point for conservation projects on the plateau.

6. Improvements could be made to some techniques – particularly the stone lines and stone bunds.

7. In spite of their efforts the Dogon need urgent assistance in the field of soil and water conservation because of the natural rate of erosion on the plateau. They need both help to improve their own techniques, and in the provision of tools.

Sana Nantoume

"I learnt these techniques from any parents. If my children learn to use these techniques I think they will benefit in the future. They should do as I do. We are not here on earth for ever, and if you don't work you won't profit. There really are advantages to using these traditional techniques".

2. PROJET LUTTE ANTI-EROSIVE (PLAE)

SUMMARY

PLAE is the largest and longest established conservation project in Mali. The project was set up under the Malian Textile Development Company in 1986 to combat the increasing problem of erosion on fields and village land. Cotton sales had increased farmers' incomes and surplus cash was used to buy more cattle. Overgrazing then caused decreased vegetative cover and therefore more runoff. An increase in erosion followed, and this finally led to poorer crop yields. PLAE introduced the concept of "village land-use management", planned and coordinated by village associations. Several erosion control techniques have been introduced – some more successfully than others. For example, live fences and tree planting on an individual basis have been very popular, whereas grazing control has been very difficult to put into practice.

Name: Projet Lutte Anti-Erosive.
Compagnie Malienne de
Developpement des Textiles (CMDT)

Contact: The Chief of Project, PLAE

Address: B.P. 01 Koutiala, Mali

Status: PLAE is a sub-unit of an Agro-Industry

Sponsor/Donor: Dutch and Malian Governments

Date of Start: 1986

BACKGROUND

Unlike most of Mali, the area where PLAE operates is not arid. There is usually enough rainfall for food crops – and also for growing cotton.

But just like elsewhere in the Sahel, there has been a reduction in rainfall over the last twenty years. The annual average in the Koutiala area has fallen from 1020mm (1931-1971) to 820mm (1972-1987).

Farmers now have two main problems. With the lower rainfall, short drought spells during the growing season have become more common. But of more concern is the violence of the rain when it does fall. During the months of July and August there is often just too much rainfall – and it is concentrated into intense showers.

The result is runoff and erosion. A single rainstorm is enough to cause severe erosion if the land is not adequately protected by a good cover of grass or crops.

The land in the area has become degraded by water and wind erosion and the problem has got much worse in recent years. Several factors have helped to accelerate the rate of degradation:

1. The human population has increased in recent years – by more than 40% between 1976 and 1987.

2. There is a growing shortage of good agricultural land. The amount of land farmed has increased enormously, partly because of the needs of the growing population, and partly as a result of the popularity of the cash crop – cotton. There is rarely a chance now to rest fields under the traditional fallow system. The soil becomes exhausted and erodes more easily.

More people need more wood for cooking... and as a result the demand for fuelwood has slipped out of balance with the supply. Only 60 years ago this area used to be a forest. Now it only produces about half of the wood that is required. Villagers have even started to cut the protected fruit and nut trees "Nere" (Parkia biglobosa) and "Karite" (Butyrospermum parkii) which grow within the fields.

Mali

Poor husbandry practices, like burning crop residues and ploughing downslope, have helped to make the erosion problem worse.

One unusual factor in the land management problem here is the success of the cotton production in the area, which has indirectly led to erosion. What has happened is as follows:

Cotton production is promoted by CMDT and the families who plant cotton can make a good income from it which is very often invested in livestock. According to PLAE there are now many more livestock in the area than the land can support. The result is severe overgrazing, leading to increased runoff from the plateaux. The runoff has in turn caused erosion on the agricultural fields, and the yield of the cotton crop has decreased.

The erosion in the cotton fields and the expressed concern of the villagers themselves convinced CMDT that action needed to be taken.

Some recommendations for better resource management had been developed by a research project [the Division of Research on Rural Production Systems (DRSPR)], which had been working on erosion control for a number of years. These were used as the basis of a programme, and PLAE – the "project which struggles against erosion" was born.

PLAE's Approach and Objectives

PLAE began operations in May, 1986. The twin objectives were:

- to halt land degradation
- to improve conditions for crop production

COTTON PRODUCTION IS PROMOTED BY CMDT

DRSPR had formulated the concept of village land-use management using a "global approach" to conservation. It had been concluded that bits and pieces of isolated activity such as earth bunding, for example, would not answer the overall problem.

The recommendation was to introduce a programme of conservation measures designed to protect the whole watershed from the plateaux at the top, to the valleys at the bottom. The programme would be introduced in phases, starting with communal work at the top of the watershed and ending with conservation on the actual fields. This was the approach which PLAE adopted.

After studying the profile of a typical watershed (see technical section) the village land was divided into three zones, each requiring different management systems. These were called:

1. Sylvo-pastoral zone (firewood and grazing);
2. Cultivated zone (cropped fields);
3. "Protection zone" (grazing land which is degraded).

In summary the problems are:

- a large, and growing population
- a greatly expanded farmed area under the cash crop, cotton
- a shortage now of good land
- heavy, intense rainfall in certain months
- a fuelwood shortage leading to deforestation
- overstocking of cattle and consequent overgrazing
- poor traditional cultivation practices making erosion worse
- decreasing crop yields due to reduced soil fertility.

60

Suitable techniques were designed for each.

ACTIVITIES AND TECHNIQUES

The main function of PLAE is to provide training for the staff of CMDT and the villagers.

Once the process of motivation and training is well underway in the villages, the Village Associations take responsibility for coordinating the programme and putting the various techniques into practice.

During its first three year phase, PLAE has helped more than 20 villages, but has concentrated on the typical cotton-growing village of Kaniko. Here the full range of conservation techniques has been tested. Some of the techniques, like stone bunds, have a direct effect on conservation, while others have an indirect effect – for example improved cooking stoves.

Some of the measures could be used in the drier areas of sub-Saharan Africa, for example improved cattle pens. Others are particularly suited to the climatic and economic conditions of this part of southern Mali, for example tied ridging.

The measures are as follows:

Protection of the Plateaux

Grazing control on the plateaux is essential to give the vegetation a chance to recover. However this requires communal agreement, and has so far met with little success – partly because the law allows anyone to graze livestock on the common land, and anyone can cut wood if a fee is paid to the government.

Earth Bunds/Waterways

The original plan was to build earth bunds to lead runoff from the plateaux into waterways between fields. But in practice bunds broke and the waterways led to gullying. The technique was soon replaced in most places by...

Stone Bunds

Stone bunds sited just above the fields slow and filter the runoff. There is no need then for a waterway, and this has proved a better way of protecting fields. Stones are transported by the farmers' donkey carts – which have proved cheaper than transport by lorries and just as efficient. Work is carried out by village groups.

Live Fences

LIVE FENCE OF EUPHORBIA

Live fences around farmers' fields only give a limited amount of protection against erosion – mainly by filtering out sediment from runoff. Their main purpose is keeping out livestock and they are popular!

Grass Strips

Broad strips of grass across the slope in farmers' fields act as living barriers to runoff. These have been reduced in size and spaced further apart since the original design because farmers felt they took up too much space. Lack of suitable grass seed has been another problem.

Check Dams

Gullies in fields are stabilised by small check dams of stone or branches. When built carefully, these can be make a difference very quickly.

Tree Planting

Communal tree planting in the form of village woodlots has not been as popular or as easy to organise as tree planting by individuals. The project has now changed its emphasis towards planting at the farm or household level by individuals.

Cultivation Practices/Tied Ridging

Conservation farming techniques have not been fully adopted. However most farmers now plough across the slope as recommended. A special ox-drawn implement which makes tied ridges is being introduced. But most farmers still have to make earth ties in the furrows by hand – which is time consuming and therefore not very popular.

Improved Cattle Pens

IMPROVED CATTLE PEN

The traditional cattle pens have been increased in size. Stems and leaves from crops are thrown in to be trampled and mixed with manure to form a rich and bulky compost. This is spread on the fields and helps to maintain fertility.

Improved Stoves

Improved low cost cooking stoves are 30% more efficient in terms of fuelwood usage than conventional stoves. Stoves are made locally from earth, and save women some of the time and labour involved in collecting firewood. This programme began in 1987, and up to 1989 more than 6,000 stoves have been made.

PROJECT MANAGEMENT AND ORGANISATION OF WORK

Management of the Project:

PLAE has its headquarters at Koutiala, where a small team of specialist trainers are based. These trainers run technical courses for CMDT's extension staff. The village associations are motivated and trained in better conservation methods by PLAE and by the CMDT staff. However, since 1983 the number of extension staff has been reduced in this area and because they have several other duties related to cotton growing, it is not always easy for them to give enough time to PLAE activities.

Organisation of Conservation Work:

CMDT is handing over increasing responsibility to the village associations for the management of cotton production and general development. Village associations were set up by CMDT several years ago to assist with activities such as cotton marketing. In Kaniko, the village where PLAE concentrated its early interventions, the village association was set up in 1979.

Village associations are responsible for conservation of all land within each village and it is PLAE's hope is that they will eventually accept full responsibility for the management and development of their own territory. Within each village association, there is a development committee which controls technical teams, each of which is responsible for a particular task. For example, one team is responsible for surveying and lays out contours with a water tube level. Technical teams also direct group work and record achievements.

The village association helps organise working groups: it has been found that, for communal work, large groups are very difficult to organise on a regular basis. Small groups of people who know each other work better than large units!

IMPROVED STOVE

Incentives:

PLAE does not, at present, use incentives to encourage conservation work. They are considered to be unnecessary because the people in this region are relatively well-off. Also, people are given credit for farm inputs under CMDT, the amount owed being deducted from payments for cotton.

Participation:

Because the village associations are the focus for conservation activities, local participation in planning and implementation has been assured. PLAE's objective is to help the associations to take control of their own development. However experience shows that it will take a number of years to achieve this fully, particularly with the more complicated issues such as grazing management.

Extension and Training:

PLAE sees itself as a training programme. Specific technical training is given to CMDT extension staff during intensive in-service training courses. Villagers are motivated and trained in better conservation methods by means of the "GRAAP" method. This is an interactive system of training based on the use of "flannelgraphs", where cut out pieces of cloth are stuck on a felt screen. Stories can be built up on the screen by the villagers – the process of erosion, for example, can be illustrated.

This process is combined with a tour of village land by a delegation of extension agents in the company of the villagers. This has proved to be a very effective system in teaching the villagers about land use planning.

Slide shows are also used. There are two sequences of slides – one for staff training, and one for the villagers. The sequences show the whole cycle of erosion and degradation, followed by the planning process and then conservation measures put into practice.

Written material for training villagers is in the local language, Bambara. Demonstration and experimental plots are also used for extension.

YIELDS AND BENEFITS

There are no precise figures yet for the benefits of the different conservation measures in terms of yield improvements.

However, it is estimated that cotton yields can be raised from the current average of about 1,300 kg/ha to 2,000 kg/ha if a programme of conservation measures is adopted. Likewise, sorghum and millet yields would probably rise from the current 800-900 kg/ha to 1,000 kg/ha or above.

COTTON BEING WEEDED AND RIDGED

63

WOMEN NEED TO BE BROUGHT MORE INTO THE PROCESS OF DECISION MAKING

Women's Role

Women still only occupy a background role in the village associations. For example, only two out of 17 members in Kaniko's Development Committee are women. Women need to be brought more into the process of decision making.

Monitoring and Evaluation

PLAE does not yet have as much information as it would like to be able to measure the effect of each conservation technique. This is essential to be able to show which techniques work best!

PROBLEMS OUTSTANDING: WHERE NOW?

Popularity of Measures

The best accepted of the measures have been ones which can be carried out on an individual basis. Examples are the live fences around private fields and tree planting near the homestead. Several techniques – especially those which require communal action – have not gone further than the pilot phase. It is proving much more difficult to organise group work on communal land than individual work on private land.

Workload

There is already a heavy work load on the villagers for whom cotton is a six-month activity. There is a need to develop and emphasise less labour intensive techniques.

Village Land Use Management

Physical conservation measures are the framework for the programme. But until there is a change in attitude by the villagers to the use of fuelwood and grazing land there will still be a major challenge for the project. However a change in attitude is difficult to foresee with the present laws on the use of communal land.

LESSONS AND CONCLUSIONS

1. Land degradation is not only a problem in the drier, poorer areas of the Sahel! Even in this relatively prosperous zone where there is a profitable cash crop, there are serious problems of over-grazing, fuelwood supply and erosion.

2. The technical answers to conservation in a relatively wet area may be different from the drier zones, but the basic approach by a conservation project should be similar.

3. Village land-use management is a new idea in Mali. Village land-use management looks for solutions for each of the land use categories – and the village as a whole is responsible for putting them into practice. PLAE's experience will be of interest for all of Mali.

4. The project may have been over-optimistic. Several of the technical research recommendations have not proved workable in the reality of village life.

5. Flexibility is very important! PLAE has been prepared to alter techniques where necessary. For example earth bunds with waterways, which was an unpopular and unsound technique has been replaced by a much more appropriate system of stone bunding.

6. A change of attitude by villagers towards more responsibility for the environment may take years to achieve – especially with the current legislation on use of common land. Strong local institutions like the village associations supported by PLAE are needed to take the lead in communal resource management.

7. The measures which have been adopted most quickly are those which are cheap, do not take up productive land, and are implemented on an individual basis. Groups can work here – but only small informal groups of family and friends!

8. Mechanised transport of stone is not always more efficient than donkey carts – as PLAE's experience has shown.

9. The "GRAAP" system of motivation and training combined with the slide sequences have proved very effective.

10. Remaining problems include the need to improve monitoring and to increase the representation of women in decision making.

Mahamadou Laryea Cissé
Extension Worker

"In the places which had no vegetation cover there has been a regeneration since we started the various conservation measures, and in the parts of the fields where there were gullies, the gullies have been healed by the farmers' action after one or two years. There are many measures adopted here which you can really say have improved matters."

PART THREE

Technical Section

HOW STONE BUNDS ARE BUILT

1. Eroded or abandoned land is selected for treatment.

2. Contours for the bunds are surveyed using a water tube level starting at the top of the field and working downwards.

3. Lines are marked on the ground with a hoe.

4. A shallow foundation trench is dug for each bund.

5. Construction begins with large stones in the rear of the trench (downslope side).

FIG 1: CONTOUR STONE BUNDS

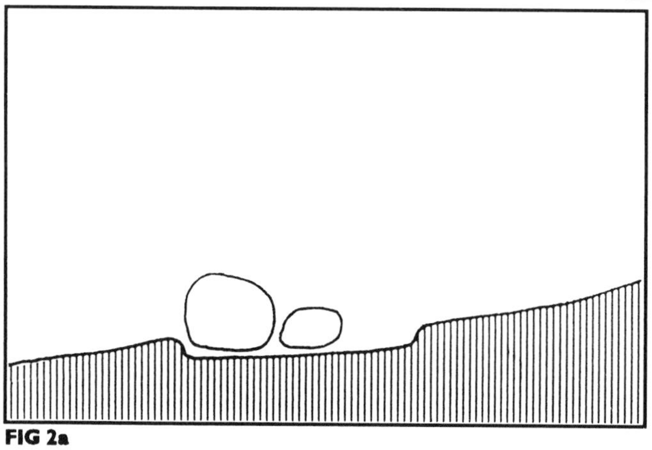

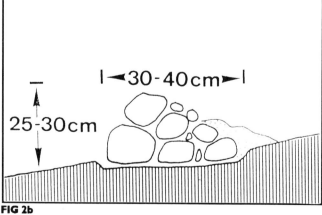

FIG 2a

6. Smaller stones are used to build the rest of the bund. The stones must be packed carefully, especially at the bottom.

8. If the land treated is an abandoned plot, the stone bunds are left for a year to catch sediment. Cultivation begins only in the second season.

FIG 2c

9. Andropogon grasses and tree seedlings are planted alongside the bund during the rains.

|◄30-40cm►|

25-30cm

FIG 2b

7. Earth from the trench is piled up in front of the bund.

Measurements

STONE BUNDS:

Spacing: 15 – 30 metres apart
Bund: 25-30cm high and 30-40 cm wide at base
Foundation trench: 5cm deep, 30-40cm wide

FIG 3: ZAI

ZAI – (PLANTING PITS)

- *zai* are deep planting pits, which help crop growth
- they are dug before the rainy season
- compost or manure is placed in the *zai* to improve fertility
- *zai* fill up with rainwater runoff during the rains

Where stone bunds and *zai* can be used:

- suitable for all dry areas
- soils do not need to be deep
- best water harvesting effect on slopes below 2%
- must be a good local supply of stone!

Measurements

ZAI

Spacing: 90cm apart
Size: 30cm diameter; 15-20cm deep
Labour: (stone bunds only) approx. 50-100 person-days/hectare

HOW TO MAKE A COMPOST PIT

1. A mud wall of not more than 50cm high is built around a pit about 75cm deep. The area enclosed should be 3 metres x 6 metres.

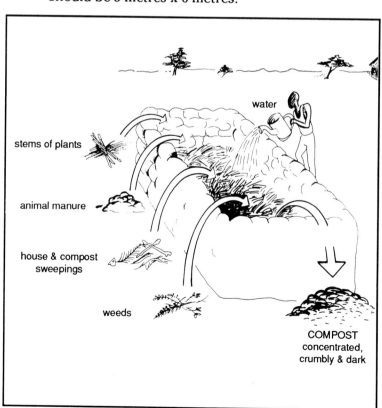

stems of plants

water

animal manure

house & compost sweepings

weeds

COMPOST
concentrated, crumbly & dark

FIG 4: COMPOST PIT

2. A layer of thin branches or stalks of cereals is placed at the bottom of the pit to for allow circulation of air, which is necessary for good composting.

3. The pit is built up with waste materials, for example:
- weeds
- stalks (well chopped)/ leaves from harvested plants
- kitchen waste
- household sweepings

4. Some old, well rotted compost and manure should be added to help the composting process to get going.

5. The pit must be kept moist by watering, and must be turned occasionally.

6. When the compost is well rotted (black and crumbly) it is ready for use – in *zai* for example. One pit makes enough for a handful or two of compost in the *zai* of 2-3 hectares.

7. Usually each pit is filled and emptied for use once each year.

HOW PERMEABLE ROCK DAMS ARE BUILT

1. The site for the permeable rock dam is identified by the village committee.

2. The most suitable sites are where gullies are beginning to form in the middle of productive land.

3. Where possible a series of permeable rock dams should begin at the top of a valley.

4. Sites immediately above gully heads should be avoided – because the permeable rock dams may be undercut.

5. If the gully which the dam crosses is less than one metre deep, no spillway is required.

6. Where a spillway is needed – to allow passage of heavy flows – it can be made from gabion baskets (wire cages filled with stone), where available.

7. Using a water tube level, the alignment of the main "wings" of the dam is marked out. The wings approximately follow the contour, and therefore they curve back down the valley.

8. A shallow foundation is dug in places where the

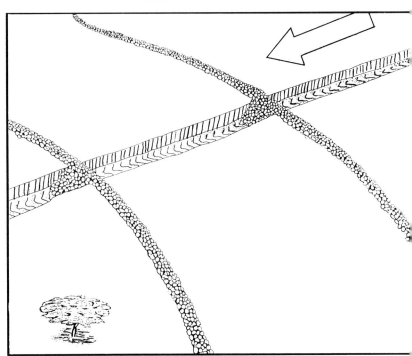

FIG 5: PERMEABLE ROCK DAMS

lessen the damage if an early flood occurs. The top is surveyed with the water tube level to make sure it is level.

Where Permeable Rock Dams can be used:

- Suitable in dry areas with less than 700mm rainfall
- Where gullies are forming in productive land
- Slopes should be less than 2%
- Good supply of stone and transport are essential

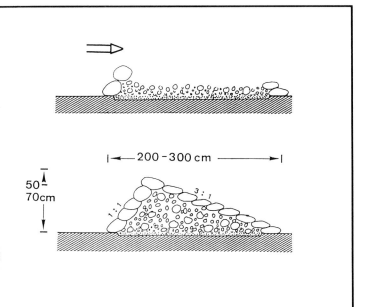

FIG 6: CONSTRUCTION OF PERMEABLE DAM

soils are easily eroded. The trench is filled with small stones/ gravel. The main dam wall is constructed carefully, using large flat stones as the casing, with smaller stones packed inside.

9. The wall is constructed evenly along its length to

Measurements:

Spacing: 50-200m apart (ideally the top of one should be level with the bottom of the one upslope but in practice, this is not usually possible)
Dam wall: 50-70cm high, 200-300cm base width
Side slopes: 3:1 downslope / 1:1 upslope

Labour/ Transport:

Stone required (for a dam 600m long): 300-600 cubic metres (depending on height)
Transport of stones by lorry: 25-40 cubic metres per day (= 50-75 tonnes)
Labour for construction: approx one person/ half cubic metre stone/ day
Labour for collection of stone and filling lorry: approx one person/half cubic metre stone/ day

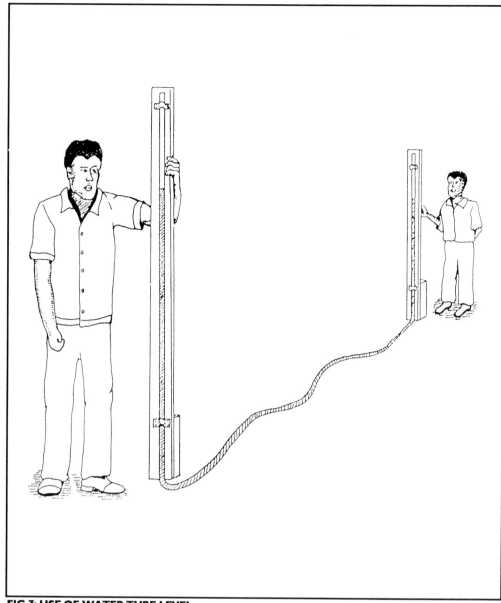

FIG 7: USE OF WATER TUBE LEVEL

1. The team begins at the top of the field, and continues downslope. Two operators are necessary to hold the poles, and a third is required to trace the line on the ground with a hoe.

2. One operator ("A") remains stationary holding one pole, while the other, ("B") moves up and down the slope with the other pole until the level of water in each tube matches the "level" mark. The two points are now on the contour.

3. The person with the hoe marks the ground between the poles.

4. Operator "A" now picks up his/her pole and moves to the other side of "B" who remains stationary. It is now "A"s turn to find the correct spot.

USE OF THE WATER TUBE LEVEL FOR SURVEYING

- The water tube level is a simple surveying instrument which is used for laying out contours in fields. It is easy to understand, and farmers can quickly learn how to operate it for themselves.

- It consists of:
  – 10-20m of clear plastic piping, with inside diameter 6-10mm
  – two poles of 1.5 -2.0 metres length
  – four rubber straps (from inner tube) to attach pipe to poles
  – one to two litres of water

- The water tube level is assembled by uncoiling the tube and then filling it with water by siphoning (sucking one end of the tube with the other end dipped in water). Each end of the tube is then tied to one pole.

- The poles are held side by side and the levels of water marked on the poles.

5. This procedure is carried on until the end of the field is reached. The distance to the next contour line is paced out, and surveying continues.

6. The true contour can now be "smoothed" by eye to make ploughing easier.

> ## Important Points to Remember:
>
> - work while it is cool – heat causes the tubes to stretch
> - mark the levels again if the water spills
> - make sure the poles are held vertically
> - don't put the poles in hollows or on lumps in the field

Technical Section

71

HOW A FARM IS CONSERVED USING FANYA-JUU TERRACES

1. The farm is surveyed by a technician to see if a cutoff drain is required above the fields.

2. A cutoff drain is laid out along the contour. All the runoff from outside the farm is held and infiltrates.

3. The soil dug out from the cutoff drain is heaped downslope.

4. Contours are then surveyed with a line level.

5. Soil is loosened with hoes or mattocks along the line of the contour and then thrown upslope to make the bund. A small step is left between the

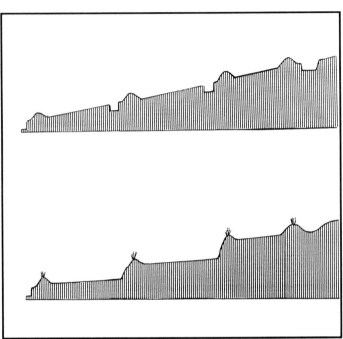

FIG 9: DEVELOPMENT OF FANYA-JUU TERRACES

7. Ploughing, weeding and natural soil movement cause the land between the terrace banks to level off into benches after a few years.

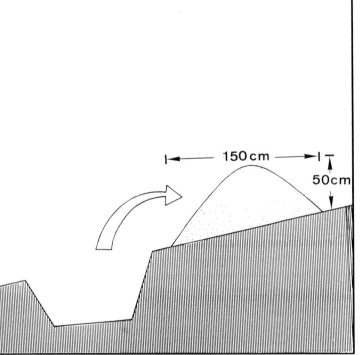

FIG 8: CONSTRUCTION OF FANYA-JUU TERRACE

trench and the bund so that soil is not washed straight back in when it rains.

6. Grass is planted on top of the bund to stabilise it. "Bana grass" is one of the best varieties for Kenya. Bananas or other trees may be planted in the trench.

FIG 10: FANYA-JUU TERRACES

72

Where fanya-juu terraces can be used

- in marginal/ wetter zones (700mm rainfall and above)
- soils should be deep
- suitable for slopes from less than 5% to 50%

Measurements

CUTOFF DRAIN:

Ditch: 1.25 m wide at top and 1.0 metre wide at bottom
Depth: approx. 1.0 metre
Gradient: usually sited on contour, but sometimes sited on a slight gradient when it is joined to a natural waterway

FANYA-JUU TERRACE

Spacing of terrace banks:
usually between 5 and 20 metres apart, (depends on the slope of the land – the steeper the land, the closer the terrace banks)
Trench: 60cm wide and 60cm deep
Bund: 50cm high and 150cm wide at base
Step: 20cm between trench and bund
Gradient: sited on contour (in dry areas)
Labour: 150-350 person-days/ hectare (for cutoff and terraces)

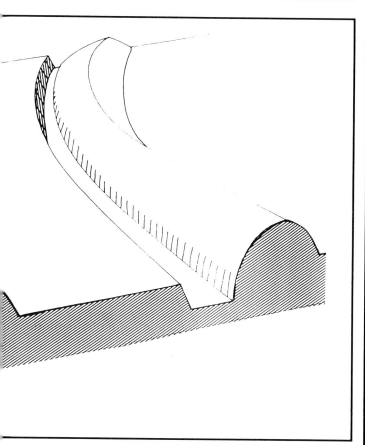

OTHER CONSERVATION TECHNIQUES USED IN MACHAKOS

Conservation Farming

"Conservation farming" means reducing erosion by good crop husbandry. This includes:
- contour ploughing
- correct spacing
- strip cropping (alternating strips of different crops)
- use of farm yard manure and fertilisers.

FIG II: CONTOUR PLOUGHING

Grass Strips

Grass strips are a cheap alternative to fanya-juu terracing. A grass like "Makarikari" (Panicum coloratum) is planted in dense strips, up to a metre wide, along the contour. The grass slows down runoff and silt builds up in front of the strip. Benches are formed, though this takes a long time to occur.

Gully Control

Gully control is expensive and therefore not usually a priority, except where gullies threaten good land, roads or buildings. Gullies are stabilised by the use of a variety of materials, including brushwood held in place by stakes of wood from trees which sprout from cuttings (eg Commiphora spp.).

Technical Section

73

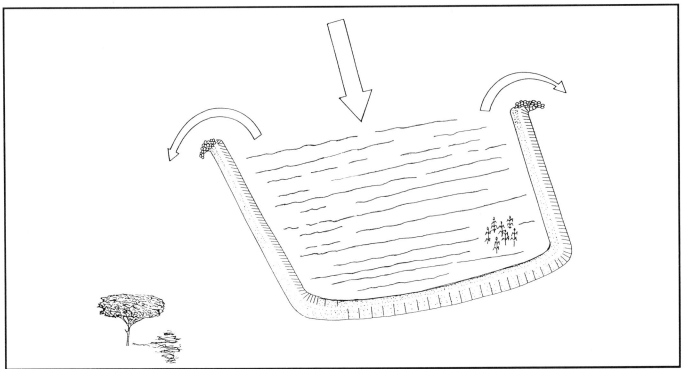

FIG 12: RAINWATER HARVESTING GARDEN

HOW A RAINWATER HARVESTING GARDEN IS MADE

1. A suitable site for the garden is chosen – this is where a small gully brings rainwater runoff to the plot.

2. Starting from the centre of the plot, a line level is used to survey the land before levelling (see next section).

3. The position of the "bottom" bund and the side bunds are pegged out after discussions between plot owner and technician.

4. The outline of the bund's cross section is marked with stakes and string to guide construction.

5. Oxen scoops are used to level the plot and to collect soil for construction.

6. Soil is carried in basins, and layer by layer the bunds are compacted by foot.

7. The line level is again used to make sure the top of the bund is level around the whole plot, and that the tips of the side bunds are on the same contour.

8. The tips of the side bunds are then protected from erosion by covering with loose stone.

9. Where too much runoff from the catchment is a problem, a diversion ditch is made to prevent runoff entering the field.

Where a Rainwater Harvesting Garden can be used:

- only suitable for the driest areas (less than 400mm rainfall)
- deep soils necessary
- soil should not be a "cracking clay"
- slopes less than 2%

Measurements

Plot size: 0.5 – 2.0 hectares
Earth moved: 500-1000 cubic metres per hectare
Maximum depth of flooding (before overflow around the spillway occurs): 25cm
Maximum dimensions of the bund:
height – 1 metre
base width – 8 metres
top width – one metre
sideslopes – (3 or) 4:1 downslope/ 3:1 upslope
Labour required: 250-500 person-days/ hectare
(when oxen scoop used)

USE OF THE LINE LEVEL FOR SURVEYING

- The line level is a simple instrument which is used for laying out contours and for other simple surveying tasks. It is quick to operate, accurate and easy to transport.

- A line level consists of two poles which may be short (as in Turkana) or the height of a person (as in Machakos). A notch is made in each pole at exactly the same height and one end of a length of string (usually 8 metres) is tied to each notch.

- The centre of the string is marked and a builder's spirit level is hung on the string at this point.

- When the bubble is in the middle of the spirit level, the two poles are on ground of equal elevation – that is, the two points are "level" or "on the contour".

How to Lay Out a Contour

1. Each pole is held by an operator and the line level read by a third person. The first pole is held by operator "A" who remains stationary. Operator "B" then moves up and down the slope until the level reads dead centre.

2. The two positions are marked, and while "A" moves to "B's" old position, "B" moves onwards

and the process continues until the length of contour required has been completed.

3. The true contour is then "smoothed" by eye to give a better shape for ploughing.

How to Survey Land for Levelling

1. The centre of the field is used as the starting point. A flat stone is placed in a hole with one side level with the ground surface. This is the "bench mark".

2. Operator "A" places his/her pole on this stone. "B" stands downslope with his/her pole on top of a wooden peg. The peg is driven into the ground until a level is found. The top of the peg will be above ground surface. "A" then moves the pole to this peg, and "B" continues down the field and places his/her pole on another peg.

3. The process is similar for the upslope part of the field, except that the pegs are driven below ground to find the level.

4. During the land levelling process, soil is scraped away from around the upslope pegs, and deposited around the downslope pegs. This continues until the tops of all the pegs are at the new surface level.

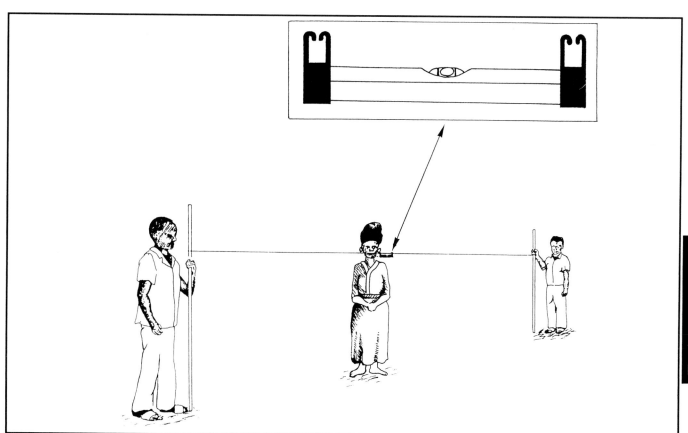

FIG 13: USE OF LINE LEVEL

MALI
1. TRADITIONAL TECHNIQUES ON THE DOGON PLATEAU

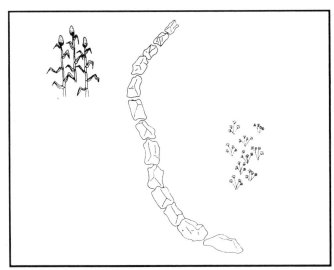

FIG 14: STONE LINES

1. STONE LINES

How They Work

- The idea of stone lines is to slow runoff and reduce erosion.

Location and Construction

- Stone lines are used very widely, on cultivated land – and also barren land which is to be used in future – where the slopes are shallow and where stones are available.
- Stone lines are placed approximately across the slope. Distance between the lines depends on availability of stones.

Measurements and Labour

- The structures often consist of just a single line of large stones, of 20-30 cm height.
- No estimates of labour requirements are available.

Improvements Possible

- Possible improvements include placing the lines on the contour, and building them slightly higher, and more carefully to avoid runoff forming small rills between them. A small foundation trench would also improve their effectiveness.

2. EARTH MOUNDS

How They Work

- The small mounds dug between plants help to slow runoff as well as acting as "mini-compost heaps", improving soil fertility.

Location and Construction

- Earth mounds are used throughout the Dogon Plateau, and also elsewhere in the drier parts of Mali.
- Mounds are constructed during the first weeding in July when weeds are scraped together and covered with earth.
- The next season's seeds are planted into what remains of the mounds – where the fertility of the soil has been improved.

Measurements and Labour

- The mounds are about 20 cm high, and are spaced between clumps of plants – often about a metre apart.
- It is estimated that it takes about 10-15 person/days to form mounds on an hectare of cropped land.

FIG 15: EARTH MOUNDS

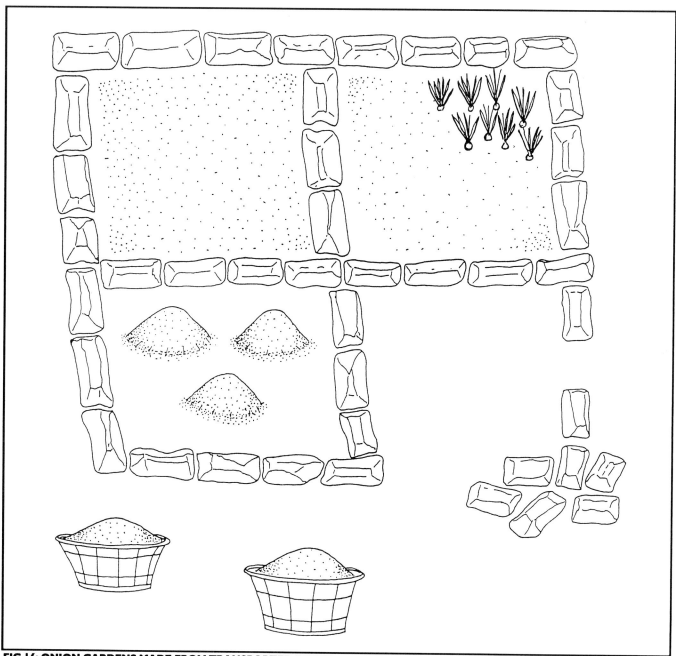

FIG 16: ONION GARDENS MADE FROM TRANSPORTED EARTH

3. ONION GARDENS
made from Transported Earth

What They Are And How They Work

- Artificial onion terraces are made by the sides of watercourses where water is available, but there is no soil.
- A network of small stone squares is built on the bare rock and after being filled with earth is planted with onions or another vegetable crop.

Construction

- The stone is brought from nearby quarries if it is not available locally.
- These squares or "terraces" are then filled with earth collected from the riverbanks and carried in baskets.
- Manure is added to the earth to make it more fertile.

Planting

- Onions or other vegetables are planted in the gardens and irrigated by hand from the nearby watersource.

Measurements and Labour

- The squares have sides of about 1 – 1.5 metres, and the soil depth is initially at least 15-20cm.
- It takes a very great deal of labour to make these gardens. One estimate is between 500 and 1,000 person/ days per hectare but it may be even more if soil and rock are not available close to the water source.

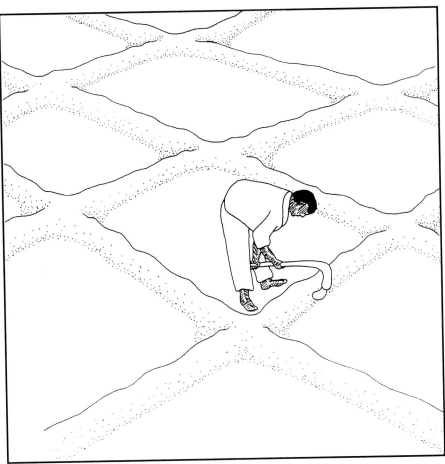

FIG 17: EARTH BASINS

4. EARTH BASINS

How They Work

- The small earth basins are intended to hold all of the rainwater which falls, therefore giving complete conservation of water and soil within the field.

Location and Construction

- Earth basins are made in agricultural fields where the soils are relatively deep.

- Construction of the basins takes place during the dry season, and they are built up later when crops are weeded.

Measurements and Labour

- Basins are made in the form of squares with each side measuring between one metre and two metres in length. The basins are largest on flatter land and smallest on more sloping land.
- Each basin is surrounded by a small earth ridge, made by a hoe, of about 15cm in height.
- This technique takes quite a large amount of work, but no accurate estimates of labour requirements are available.

2. PROJET LUTTE ANTI-EROSIVE

HOW CONSERVATION MEASURES ARE PLANNED FOR DIFFERENT LAND USE CATEGORIES

1. At the start, a cross-section or "profile" of a typical catchment in the Koutiala area was used (see fig 14) to help plan for solutions to the overall conservation problem.

2. The different land categories – plateaux, escarpments, gentle slopes etc – were then studied. From these categories, three main land use zones were identified. These zones, together with their particular problems and the technical solutions proposed are as follows:

The Cultivated Zone (a)

Location: on the gentle slopes where there are deep soils

Problems: runoff from the plateaux and escarpments causing sheet and rill erosion in agricultural fields

Conservation Techniques Recommended:
- contour stone bunds just above the fields to slow runoff from the land above

- live fences around the fields
- grass strips within the fields
- check dams made from stone or cereal stems in rills and gullies
- use of manure from the improved cattle pens in the fields – improved crop husbandry, such as tied ridging

The Protection Zone (b)

Location: the escarpments and the banks of the streams

Problems: severe erosion and deforestation

Conservation Techniques Recommended:
- protection from grazing
- revegetation with trees and grass

The Silvo-Pastoral Zone (c)

Location: the plateaux and other areas not used for cropping

Problems: lack of vegetative cover

Conservation Techniques Recommended:
- control of bush fires
- control of grazing
- control of tree cutting for fuelwood
- use of improved cooking stoves (an indirect measure)

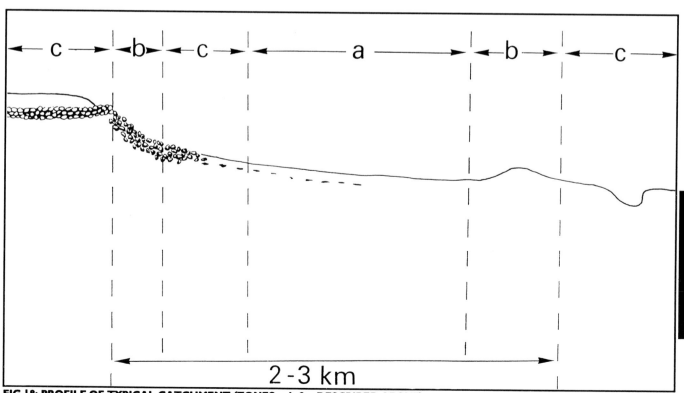

FIG 18: PROFILE OF TYPICAL CATCHMENT (ZONES a, b & c DESCRIBED ABOVE)

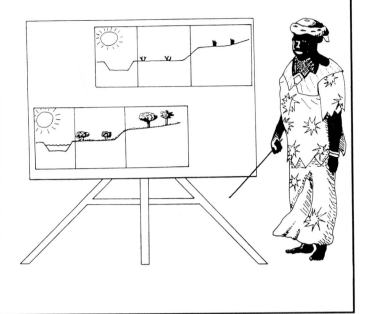

FIG 19: A FLANNELGRAPH – PART OF THE "GRAAP" METHOD

3. Villagers are involved in land-use planning by means of the "GRAAP" method of interactive training. This includes the use of "flannelgraphs" where images are stuck on a felt screen.

GRASS STRIPS

How They Work

- Grass strips are a vegetative method of erosion control.

- The strips run in a straight line across the slope, within cultivated fields.
- Runoff is slowed by the strips and silt deposited.
- Technically grass strips work well, but there have been some problems including shortage of appropriate seed, and the growth of weeds within the strips.

Planting

- The grass species planted are selected for their value as fodder as well as ground cover.
- <u>Brachiaria ruzizensis</u> has grown well, but <u>Pennisetum pedicellatum</u> proved less good for ground cover or for fodder.

Where Grass Strips are Suitable

- Grass strips such as these are most suitable for the areas with above 700mm annual rainfall, as in southern Mali.

Measurements and Labour

- The original design was for strips 5 metres wide and 50 metres apart, but farmers objected to the loss of land, so strips were reduced to 3 metres wide and spaced up to 100 metres apart.
- One person can plant about 10 metres of a grass strip in an hour (including ploughing).

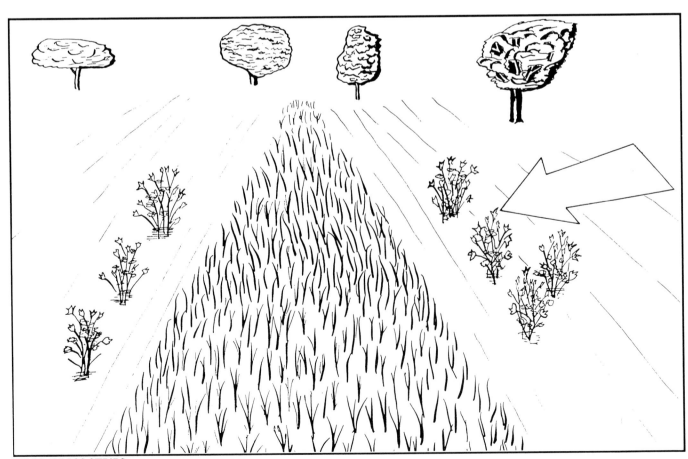

FIG 20: GRASS STRIPS

FIG 21: LIVE FENCES

LIVE FENCES

How They Work

- Live fences are planted for two reasons:
  - to protect fields from animals
  - to act as a vegetative barrier to runoff

Planting

- Cuttings of <u>Euphorbia balsimifera</u> are planted closely together to form hedges around agricultural fields.
- Other species tested have been <u>Balanites sp.</u> <u>Cajanus cajun</u>, <u>Ziziphus sp.</u> and <u>Acacia spp.</u>

- Planting takes place before the rainy season. This is because Euphorbia cuttings prefer to be planted dry. This is an advantage because labour is available at this time.
- Hedges are planted around each farmer's land and also around individual fields within it.

Where Live Fences are Suitable

- Live fences of different Euphorbia species can be used very widely in the drylands of sub-Saharan Africa.

Labour

- One person can plant about 20 metres per hour (of Euphorbia).

81

BIBLIOGRAPHY
REFERENCES AND FURTHER READING

L'Etat Actuel de la Conservation des Eaux et du Sol dans le Sahel,
Chris Reij, Free University Amsterdam, 1989

- brings together all the information that is available on the current state of different SWC programmes in the Sahel. An extensive section on PAF, and a very useful bibliography. (French)

Le Sahel en Lutte Contre la Desertification,
Rene Rochette (ed.), GTZ, Eschborn, Germany, 1989

- describes a permeable rock dam project which works in the same area as PATECORE (pages 239-261: "Rissiam/ Bam – Digues Filtrantes".

- gives a very useful overview of the PLAE project written largely by project staff. However only the early experience of the project, up to the beginning of 1988 is recorded (pages 369 – 387: "Experience No. 20, Kaniko/ Koutiala – Mali"). (French)

Mali-Sud; D'un amenagement anti-erosif des champs a la gestion de l'espace rural,
Bulletin 317, Royal Tropical Institute, Amsterdam, 1989

- a more detailed account of PLAE's activities than the previous reference, and includes more up-to-date information as well as a more thorough analysis. (in French)

Rainwater Harvesting,
Arnold Pacey with Adrian Cullis, Intermediate Technology Publications, 1986

- a book which is an excellent introduction to rainwater harvesting especially in sub-Saharan Africa. Gives information about the Agro-forestry Project amongst others. (English)

Ramblings on Soil Conservation – An Essay from Kenya,
Wilhelm Ostberg, SIDA, Sweden ISBN 91-586-7091-2

- a very enjoyable and easy to read booklet about soil conservation in Kenya. looks at socio-economic issues and is full of little stories and lessons from real life. (in English)

Soil and Water Conservation in Kenya,
Proceedings of the 3rd National Workshop, Dept. Agric. Engineering, University of Nairobi and SIDA, Nairobi, Sept. 1986

- nearly 50 papers on different aspects of soil conservation in Kenya, including Machakos and Kitui Districts. Papers are grouped into sections, for example "erosion", "conservation of croplands" and "policy planning and socio-economic aspects". (in English)

Soil and Water Conservation in Sub-Saharan Africa,
Free University Amsterdam (for IFAD/ FIDA), 1986

- an excellent report which analyses SWC in SSA and explains why so many projects have gone wrong. Refers often to PAF as an example of a successful project. (English)

82

Soil Conservation for Increased Agricultural Production,
Ministry of Agriculture, Engineering Division, P.O. Box 30028, Nairobi

- one of a large series of training booklets from MOA. This one is a cartoon booklet explaining how erosion occurs and what to do about it – including how to make "fanya-juu" terraces. Presented in easy to follow cartoon sequences. (in English)

Water Harvesting for Plant Production,
Chris Reij and others, World Bank Technical Paper No. 91, 1988

- a literature review which gives technical and socio-economic background to projects and traditional systems in Africa. Also contains a very useful bibliography. (English – French version will be coming out soon)

CONTACT ADDRESSES

Further information may be obtained from the projects themselves or the sponsoring agency/department.

PAF

The Project Coordinator
Projet Agro-Forestier
B.P. 200
Ouahigouya,
Burkina Faso

Oxfam
BP 489
Ouagadougou
Burkina Faso

LPDP

The Secretary, LPDP
Oxfam
PO Box 40680
Nairobi
Kenya

ITDG
Myson House
Railway Terrace
Rugby CV21 3HT
UK

PATECORE

The Director
PATECORE
BP 271
Kongoussi
Burkina Faso

NSWCP

The Deputy Director of Agriculture
Agricultural Engineering Division
Ministry of Agriculture
PO Box 30025
Nairobi
Kenya

PLAE

The Director
Projet Lutte Anti-Erosive
CMDT
BP 01
Koutiala
Mali

DOGON PLATEAU

Two sources of further information about the Dogon Plateau are:

Projet Hydraulique Rurale
BP 25
Bandiagara
Mali

Near East Foundation, Douentza
PO 2627
Bamako
Mali

ACKNOWLEDGMENTS
ALIN/IIED would like to thank the following for their assistance.

BURKINA FASO:

OXFAM; PROJET AMENAGEMENT DES TERROIRS ET CONSERVATION DES RESSOURCES DANS LE PLATEAU CENTRAL (PATECORE); PROJET AGRO-FORESTIER (PAF) FONDS DE L'EAU ET DE L'EQUIPEMENT RURAL (FEER); DIRECTION DE VULGARISATION AGRICOLE (DVA) PROGRAMME NATIONAL DE GESTION DES TERROIRS VILLAGEOIS (PNGTV); CENTRES REGIONAUX DE PROMOTION AGROPASTORAL (CRPA); MINISTERE DE L'ADMINISTRATION TERRITORIALE (MAT).

KENYA:

OXFAM; INTERMEDIATE TECHNOLOGY DEVELOPMENT GROUP (ITDG); LOKITAUNG PASTORAL DEVELOPMENT PROJECT (LPDP); MINISTRY OF AGRICULTURE, MACHAKOS DISTRICT; MINISTRY OF AGRICULTURE, AGRICULTURAL ENGINEERING DIVISION; SWEDISH INTERNATIONAL DEVELOPMENT AGENCY (SIDA); THE ENGLISH PRESS LTD., NAIROBI; MINISTRY OF INFORMATION AND BROADCASTING.

MALI:

OXFAM; PROJET LUTTE ANTI-EROSIVE (PLAE); COMPAGNIE MALIENNE POUR LE DEVELOPPEMENT DES TEXTILES (CMDT); PROJET HYDRAULIQUE RURALE (PHR); PROJET VULGARISATION AGRICOLE (PVA); VILLAGERS OF THE DOGON PLATEAU; DIRECTION NATIONALE DES EAUX ET FORETS; MINISTERE DE L'ENVIRONNEMENT ET DE L'ELEVAGE; MINISTERE DE L'INFORMATION.